GUINNESS:
THE STORIES BEHIND THE
RECORDS

By Norris McWhirter
&
The Editors of The
"Guinness Book of World Records"

Sterling Publishing Co., Inc. New York

FRONT COVER PICTURES, starting at top left and reading clockwise:
Steve McPeak climbing the cable car wire from Rio de Janeiro to the top of
Sugar Loaf Mountain (a Franklin Berger photo); Norris McWhirter with
world's largest cat (courtesy BBC − TV); Sandy Allen, between two Guinness
executives (courtesy Michael Hatfield); Toby Hoffman, strong man (courtesy
Toby Hoffman); Rosser Reeves ruby (courtesy Rosser Reeves); Domino tumble
(courtesy Hemophilia Foundation); Jeff Kane, pogo jumper (courtesy Jeff
Kane); Adele Millard with goat (courtesy Joan Millard); Balloon release at
Guinness Museum, Gotemba, Japan (photo by Franklin Berger). **BACK
COVER CARTOON,** courtesy of *Punch*.

Library of Congress Cataloging in Publication Data

McWhirter, Norris, 1925–
    Guinness: the stories behind the records.

    Includes index.
    1. Curiosities and wonders.   I. Guinness book of
world records.   II. Title.
AG243.M328   031′.02   81-85584
ISBN 0-8069-0244-2   AACR2
ISBN 0-8069-0245-0 (lib. bdg.)
ISBN 0-8069-7618-7 (pbk.)

For the Record

—from the editors

For more than a quarter of a century, the *Guinness Book of World Records* has been chronicling the outer limits of the universe and life on Earth, but the fact-filled book has room for little more than a brief description of each record. The Guinness staffs in London, New York, and around the world have always been aware that the details of record setting are often more extraordinary than the records themselves. This new book, the first of a projected series, provides, for the first time, an opportunity to reveal the stories behind the efforts that have fascinated so many readers. Through interviews, investigations, research and much correspondence, we have assembled a diverse collection of articles that we hope you will find entertaining and informative.

Reviewing the stories in this volume, we can readily note that records are set under a great variety of circumstances. Some records are utterly spontaneous (Les Henson was just trying to score a basket when he unleashed his record-breaking heave), and some are the products of years of planning and practice (the supersonic rocket car comes to mind). The motivations for mastering certain fields of endeavor are also very different: John Marino was trying to rehabilitate a back aliment; Jan Todd began serious training because she was certain she could break the women's powerlifting record; and Willie Hollingsworth dedicated months to learning the fine art of balancing a full milk bottle on his head specifically for a listing in Guinness.

The book is organized with spectacular stunts first, followed by sports stories, and then odd records and interesting people and events. One fact shines through all of the variety—the record-breaking competition is fierce. Judging by the stupendous volume of mail that arrives at the Guinness offices, record fever continues to rage as strongly as ever. The mail also indicates, however, that there are many misunderstandings as to Guinness' role in ratifying and publishing world records. To help clarify the situation, we have included a question-and-answer discussion of how to get into the Guinness book, and a selection of letters from among the thousands we receive.

The stories themselves will, of course, help to shed light on what is (and is not) Guinness. Mostly, however, we expect the stories to offer delightful and astounding reading about extraordinary people, places and things.

GUINNESS:
THE STORIES BEHIND THE RECORDS

(page 62)

(page 112)

(page 48)

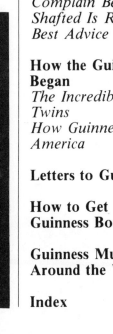

DAREDEVIL EVENT OF THE 19TH CENTURY

Frenchman, with His Manager on His Back, Walks Across and Cavorts Over Niagara Falls

The Great Blondin, 1888

Walking on tightrope across the gorge created by Niagara Falls has been the dream of many people, but the first person to achieve it was a Frenchman in the spring of 1859. His name was Jean François Gravelet, known as Blondin.

Blondin had come to America in 1855 with a group of rope walkers or funambulists under contract to P.T. Barnum, the circus owner. The Frenchman first visited the Falls in 1858, where he almost immediately became obsessed with the idea of crossing the Niagara River on a tight-rope.

Previously there had been a man who leaped from a perch 85 feet up (and later from 120 feet up) over Niagara Falls into the raging waters between the cataract on the U.S. side and Horseshoe Falls on the Canadian side.

And on Saturday, September 3, 1827, an event had brought out 10,000 witnesses. They had come to watch as a modern Noah's Ark, full of animals and birds, was sent over Horseshoe Falls. The "ark" was an old unserviceable hulk of a schooner named "Michigan" and on its decks were two bears and a buffalo; an eagle was tied fast to the vessel's mast; and on board were a goose and several other animals and birds. The hotelkeepers of the area had thought up this scheme to drum up business, bringing out morbidly curious tourists.

The "ark" was towed to a spot a half mile above the rapids and abandoned there. As Francis Petrie, the official historian of Niagara Falls, puts it, "it was sad day for all animal lovers."

The "ark" didn't go over the Falls until after it had hit a rock in the river and been broken apart. The survivors were the bears, who swam to a small island and were rescued, and the goose who was exhausted but alive and proudly taken home by a Mr. Duggan.

Now it was 1859 and Blondin was set to defy the danger of the rapids and the Falls. But there was only one suitable anchorage spot for his cable to be tied on the Canadian shore. After renting the spot at an exorbitant price, he had to purchase an 1,100-foot-long rope to span the gorge. Blondin didn't have the $1,300 necessary. Finally a Mr. Foster in New York City agreed to make a special manila rope, and a Mr. MacHamblin paid for it.

By late June 1859 the rope was stretched across the Niagara River halfway between the two Falls, about where the Whirlpool Rapids Bridge is today. Each end of the rope had 18 guy lines fastened to trees and posts, holding it steady.

Spectators were charged 25 cents to see the crossing from vantage points near the starting area on the U.S. side and, for 25 cents more one could rent a seat for the show.

June 28 was the date set. Many American and Canadian newspapers carried ads, the promoters printed posters and gave out "broadsides" announcing the event. Thousands arrived in Niagara and had to wait because for two days heavy rains fell. But on June 30 at 5 p.m., with much fanfare, Blondin set out for Canada on his tightrope with a 40-foot-long balancing pole. In the center the rope sagged of its own weight, so there was an uphill climb to the Canadian side.

Let Mr. Petrie tell the rest of the story in his own words:

A short way out, Blondin stopped, lay down full length on the rope, on his back, and then raised himself on one leg. Continuing to the halfway mark, he lowered a bottle on a string to the *Maid of the Mist* steamer in the river below, which crew members filled with wine. Hauling the bottle back up to him, Blondin drank it and went on his way.

Some reports stated the bottle contained water taken from the Niagara River, whose waters Blondin was defying.

The crossing took 20 minutes to accomplish and was the first of nine such walks that took from five to 50 minutes. Blondin's feats were daring to say the least and he did everything imaginable on his tightrope.

He walked and ran across it, forwards and backwards, in daylight and in darkness. Sometimes he had his arms and legs shackled in irons, completely enclosed in a sack with only two holes cut in it for his hands.

He rode a bicycle back and forth and one time trundled a wheelbarrow to the center of the rope where he stopped,

The famous Blondin with his agent, Harry Colcord on his back, walking across Niagara Falls in 1859.

cooked an omelet on a small stove placed in the wheelbarrow, ate part of the omelet, and lowered the rest to passengers on the *Maid of the Mist* below.

He stood on his head on the rope in midstream and again on his head on a chair balanced on the rope. Another crossing was made on stilts.

His supreme act was to carry his manager, Harry Colcord, across on his back on a special harness resting on his shoulders, with two barrel hoop iron hooks in which Colcord placed his legs.

Blondin made three such crossings with Colcord on his back, which in itself is hard to believe, but the hardest part to believe (and especially witness) were the five to seven rest periods Blondin needed in which Colcord had to get down off Blondin's back, stand on the rope behind him, and then remount.

Colcord was 35 years of age at this time and was 5 foot 2 inches tall, weighing 145 pounds, or almost as much as Blondin.

The year 1859 was so successful financially, Blondin and his manager scheduled a repeat performance for the following year. Subsequently even greater crowds, numbering into the hundreds of thousands, came by stage-

coach, steamboat and railway to view the stunts of "The Little Wonder" in 1860.

The Prince of Wales, later King Edward VII, visited Niagara Falls on September 15, 1860, and saw Blondin perform. Blondin offered to carry the Prince over the rope on his back instead of his manager, but the prince discreetly refused.

In the version of Blondin's first walk published by Philip Mason in 1969, it was reported that as he neared the Canadian shore "he paused, steadied the balancing pole, and suddenly executed a back somersault. Men screamed, women fainted. Those near the rope wept and begged him to come in. When he finally stepped off the rope he was grabbed by a delirious, shouting, crying, sobbing horde of well-wishers who escorted him to a champagne reception."

Blondin's stunts were widely acclaimed around the world as the events of the century. More than 100,000 crammed the gorge for some of the events and he made Niagara Fall even more famous.

To honor Blondin there is now a statue of him in his funambulist attire standing on a cable astraddle Clifton Hill. The bicycle and wheelbarrow which he used are on view at Tussaud's Wax Museum in Niagara Falls, Ontario, and a picture story of these events adorns the walls of the Guinness Museum on Clifton Hill today. ■

John Russell setting the world record at Madison Square Garden before a select audience.

STILT WALKING IS SCARY, SAYS RECORD SETTER

Before his 33-foot-record, John Russell set a record in Cincinnati at 31 feet.

The one principal thing is to keep moving once you start walking because if you stand still you tend to fall backwards.

High-stepping clowns perform in Ringling Bros. and Barnum & Bailey Circus, where John Russell is featured.

John Russell surpassed his own record of high stilt walking when he took 34 steps covering a distance of 16 feet on aluminum stilts weighing 40 lbs. on which his feet rested 33 feet off the ground and his 6-foot-3-inch frame caused his eyes to be almost 40 feet above the floor.

This is the interview he gave immediately afterwards to the American editor of the Guinness Book, David A. Boehm, who had witnessed the record-breaking event:

Q: How does it feel to be walking with your head 40 feet in the air?

A: Scary! My knees tremble whenever I start high stilt walking.

Q: Are you nervous because you have a fear of falling?

A: Yes. A fear of falling is always with me. But once I start moving I don't think about it.

Q: What would happen if you started to fall?

A: As you noticed in my fake start, I put my hand out and grabbed hold of the bar alongside of me.

Q: Have you ever taken a fall?

A: Yes. I fell once in Biloxi, Mississippi, when my 24-foot-high stilts slipped on wet cement.

Q: Did you hurt yourself?

A: No, I was caught by the performance director.

Q: Did you get right back up on the stilts or were you afraid to climb up again?

A: I was shaking all over that day and the next. But two days later I traveled to Mobile, Alabama, and was ready to go on with the show, and I never fell again.

Q: You must like heights or else you wouldn't be doing this.

A: Yes, that's right. I love flying in airplanes and even when I was a kid I loved to dive off a cliff into Green Lake which is near my home town, Appleton, Wisconsin.

Q: How old are you and when did you start on stilts?

A: I'm 26 now and I started when I was 21. In those 5 years I performed on stilts that were 10, 12 and 13 feet high going up all the way to 15 feet. When I perform in the Circus generally I use 12-foot stilts. I figure that in these 5 years I have been in 550 shows a year working most of the time twice a day and with practice and everything else I have been on stilts 5,885 times.

Q: Are there any secrets to walking on stilts?

A: The one principal thing is to keep moving once you start walking because if you stand still you tend to fall backwards.

Q: Do you know that you are in the Guinness Book?

A: Of course. It's my proudest achievement. In fact, for many years I wanted to meet any record-holder in the book and finally I met Marco Canestrelli who performs with me in the Circus and who holds the record for septuple twisting back somersaults.

Q: Your record in the 1981 edition of the Guinness Book, which is in the newly verified section of the back, is for walking on 31-foot stilts a total of 30 steps.

A: Yes, and then in Cincinnati, I did 36 steps on 32-foot stilts and now I am very pleased that I could make 34 steps on the 33-foot stilts.

Q: I understand that you make your own stilts. Right?

A: Yes, I design and construct them out of 16-gauge aluminum tubing, and I reinforce them at various levels and the footrests too with 3 cable struts on a triangular frame of aluminum. The big stilts weigh 35-40 lbs.

Q: I understand that you began at Clown College at Ringling Brothers.

A: Yes. I broke my arm while I was training there and I graduated with my arm in a sling.

Q: Do you dress up as a clown when you appear on stilts at the circus?

A: Yes. I think people expect performers in the Circus to look like clowns.

Q: Do you have any advice for young people who want to become circus performers?

A: I would like to advise them the way my parents wisely told me when I began, "Whatever you do, do your best." ∎

Jeff Kane at the firehouse where he broke the pogo-stick jumping record and earned a place in the "Guinness Book of World Records." (Note the man seated at the table with a log book and his finger on a counter.)

THE HUMAN KANGAROO: GATORADE, GUTS & GRANOLA

How Jeff Kane of Oak Lawn, Illinois, Convinced Guinness that He Was the New Pogo-Stick Jumping Champion

How Guinness Verifies Records:

The U.S. Editors of the Guinness Book of World Records *are always being called upon to answer questions concerning verification of record attempts. How do we verify the materials that are sent in to the New York Headquarters by the thousands every year? How do we know when we have the "real thing?"*

Over the years Guinness investigators have learned many tricks to prove the validity of a claim. Tricks not unlike the ones a detective would use when investigating a case.

Based on knowledge obtained from checking legitimate claims, we know just what does and does not happen in a record attempt.

In most cases, lack of understanding of the requirements for submitting a claim is what keeps people from getting into the book. It's unfortunate, because these people spend a great deal of time and work very hard to get into the GBWR. However, some submissions are just plain skulduggery—an attempt to deceive, and that is where our long-time experience comes in. And, we are proud to say, in that department, we are 100% successful.

The following questions are an example of the kind of questions we ask a potential recordbreaker.

We contacted Jeff Kane, a legitimate recordholder. Jeff's imagination and determination made him an outstanding candidate for entry and a fine example of how getting into the book can really happen. We were happy to give Jeff a place in the 1981 edition of the Book and as of this writing his position remains unchallenged and appears in the 1982 edition as well.

Jeff proved to us beyond question, that he jumped 120,715 jumps in 16 hours and 12 minutes, breaking Michael Barban's record of 105,338 jumps in 18 hours by making more jumps in less time.

GUINNESS: *Jeff, your submission looks very professional. What preparations did you make before starting your attempt to break the pogo stick jumping record?*

JEFF: I made sure, first of all, that I had good equipment. That's very important. I used a Master Pogo Stick, the best that's made. I started out with a brand new stick and had an extra one handy just in case something happened to the one I was using.

Jeff Kane at home after his victorious record-breaking attempt.

G: *Where did you jump?*
JEFF: I chose the Oak Lawn fire station.
G: *Why there?*
JEFF: The area is big enough to give me room and I could be on public display the whole time. Also, I needed unbiased adult witness of standing in the commuity, so the Fire Chief and other firemen were there. They took turns doing the counting. The Mayor of Oak Lawn came in to watch too.
G: *Who stayed with you through the night?*
JEFF: My mom and our next door

neighbor, Mrs. Elmore Harker, the Fire Chief's wife. They also took turns counting.
G: *How did they keep track of your jumps?*
JEFF: They used a counting machine. I have a photograph of me jumping and one of the firemen sitting at a table watching me and using the machine.
G: *What did you eat during your attempt?*
JEFF: Granola bars and Gatorade. I thought it would be best to eat light food.
G: *How did your pogo stick hold up during all of this jumping?*
JEFF: Pretty good. It got a little squeeky and we tried to squirt oil on it as I was jumping but that didn't work too well. It just made a mess of my pants legs. I also sent for extra tips to the manufacturer which I had ready because we were afraid that the jumping might wear the tip out.
G: *In your documentation you sent us a newspaper article from the Southtown Economist, your local newspaper. Did you have trouble getting other papers to cover this event?*
JEFF: No. When I called them they were interested, but said they would only come down if they had exclusive rights. I agreed and that's why I only had one newspaper cover the story.
G: *Did you get bored or depressed or discouraged?*
JEFF: Yes. When I was bored I jumped over to the TV set and tried to watch. Late at night though, I got discouraged but my mom and Mrs. Harker kept encouraging me and helped me keep my spirits up. In the daytime my friends came by and cheered me on.

As you can see, these questions, along with the documentation that Jeff sent and the contacting of witnesses by the office in England, convinced us that Jeff deserved his hard-earned place in the GBWR. ■

BEVO FRANCIS SAVED A COLLEGE WITH HIS BASKETBALL RECORDS

To ask you to believe the story of Bevo Francis is to expect you to accept a story that is much like a fairy tale. Even Hollywood does not produce fiction that is so unbelievable. It is a story of a small-town boy who saved a little college in southern Ohio from extinction, bringing the college into national prominence and money. It is the story of a shy youngster who set national basketball records almost 30 years ago that have not been beaten, and have not even been closely challenged—they were so astounding.

Clarence (Bevo) Francis averaged nearly 50 points a game in his brief college career in the early 1950's. He scored 113 points in one game—more than any other pro or collegian before or since. And he did it after playing only one season of basketball in high school.

When Francis entered Rio Grande College, the school had an archaic gymnasium that seated 150 fans. The school had just one playworthy basketball. Hardly anybody in America had heard of the tiny school, and most people wrongly pronounced the name of the college REE-O like the river in Texas rather than RY-O as the town's residents preferred.

When Francis began playing there, the crowds were as small as 62 and one night the gate receipts were $19.20. The next season, Francis's last as an amateur, the school played in Madison Square Garden in New York City and pulled in gates of as much as $35,000 and crowds of more than 13,000.

The Francis legend began in 1932 when he was born and nicknamed "Beeve" after a soft drink. "Beeve" became "Bevo" as he grew up. As a youngster he had to miss a couple of years of school because of illness. Then he transferred from one high school to Wellsville High, and couldn't play until he was a junior. As a senior he was ineligible again because he was already 20 years old. But in his single high school season, he was already a 6-foot-9-inch player with an uncanny eye for the basket. He scored 57 points in one game (one shy of the Ohio State record) and averaged over 31. Some 63 colleges wanted him.

But Bevo decided to follow a man named Newt Oliver, who had helped him polish his skills at Wellsville. Oliver had once been national scoring leader for little Rio Grande and now he was being beckoned back to the college at its darkest moment. Oliver was informed upon taking the job that the school was in a financial mess and probably would fold. There were only 92 students there when Oliver and Francis arrived and the basketball facilities consisted of a gym that was built in 1917 and one— only one—ball. Appropriately, the ball had a lump in it.

That was in 1952. Because Rio Grande was an unknown at the time, the Ohio college conference made an exception that allowed Francis, who was a couple of courses short of high school graduation, to finish his high school work and begin college concurrently.

Before long, not only did the Ohio

conference know about him, but so did the whole nation. Rio Grande players unselfishly fed the ball to their big man in an effort to draw the nation's attention, which in turn would earn the school better competition in bigger arenas—where the money was. But as a freshman, Bevo had to play in a slate of 39 games that was padded with equally unknown schools plus several teams from junior colleges and the armed services.

Bevo was awesome right from the start, when he scored 44 points against an alumni team. In his third game—against Sue Bennett College of Kentucky—he scored 58. A couple of weeks later he poured in 69 one night against Wilberforce, a four-year school. Within a short time, he upped his personal record to 72, then 76. And then on January 9, 1953, he performed the unbelievable. That night against Ashland Junior College of Kentucky, Bevo rang up 61 points in the first three quarters. Then in the final 10 minutes he dumped in 55 points for a total of 116!

It was only midseason and Bevo was averaging over 50 points. More important, little Rio Grande was in the headlines all over the nation. Big New York magazines and television networks were scurrying to Rio Grande, Ohio, to see the phenom who scored 116 and the team that scored 150 in a single game. Interestingly enough, the previous high of 87 points was also by a Rio Grande player back in 1941.

Little did they know that Bevo's wife washed uniforms for the team

Bevo Francis drives for the basket against Adelphi College at New York City's Madison Square Garden. Francis' scoring ability attracted large crowds to Rio Grande College's basketball games.

and the school couldn't even afford to pay for hamburgers when the Rio Grande Redmen played out-of-town games.

Before the year was over, Rio Grande was taking in money like mad as its games were switched to big arenas in cities like Dayton and Cleveland. And the Redmen went undefeated to set a record of 39 straight in a season. Bevo himself had an unheard-of total of 1,954 points and a 50.1 average to smash all records by far. Not bad for a freshman!

Bevo's success story may have been too impressive for his own good, though. The National Collegiate Athletic Association ruled after that season that it would only count Bevo's games against four-year, degree-granting colleges. That meant only 12 of the 39 teams on the Rio Grande schedule were recognized and Bevo's achievements were altered drastically. The 116-point outburst versus Ashland Junior College was wiped out and his average for the 12 games was cut to 48.1.

But Bevo and his teammates had succeeded in attracting enough attention to get a real national schedule for the 1953-54 campaign. Little Rio Grande was booked against such major powers as Villanova, Wake Forest, Miami, Providence, and Creighton, to name a few. And the big arenas in Boston, Philadelphia, Buffalo, Miami, Indianapolis , and Cincinnati begged the Redmen to come and play. Before Bevo's two-year career came to an end, he played before paying crowds totaling 244,000.

Surprisingly, Rio Grande held its own against the big powers. It lost to Villanova by only a point as Bevo scored 39. The game after that, Bevo scored 41 as the Redmen upset Providence. Along the line there were upsets of Miami, Wake Forest, Butler, and Creighton. Bevo was getting his usual share of points as he managed to average 46.4 points in 27 games.

But the highlight of the year and his most notable record came at mid-season when the Redmen played Hillsdale College of Michigan on a neutral court in Jackson, Ohio, on February 2, 1954. Bevo got off to his best start since the Ashland game of the previous year. By halftime he already had 43 points and was driving dizzy the three men assigned to guard him. In the second half he went wild, scoring 70 points. For the night he made 38 field goals and converted on 37 of 42 free throws—a record in itself that may never be broken in competition. Bevo's total was 113 points and this time against a four-year school. No one has come close to that record.

As the season came to a close, Bevo was hampered by injury and illness. The Redmen lost seven of their 28 games. Bevo also was concerned about his wife and child—money was scarce despite the fact that the school was coming out of the red. He decided to forego the rest of his career, cutting short the possibility of setting astronomical all-time records. He turned pro on a team to be coached by Oliver.

Bevo was good with the touring pros but the opposition wasn't good enough and he finally played out his career in a minor league until 1962. Then he went back to a small Ohio town to eke out a living as a steel-mill worker. Suddenly basketball's greatest legend was a mortal again. ∎

BASKETBALL'S LONG SHOT CONTROVERSY INVESTIGATED

Photo courtesy of Virginia Tech

Les Henson takes a conventional shot against Cincinnati. A fuss was made over the fact that the left-handed-shooting Henson had made his famous long shot with his right hand, until it was revealed that he regularly throws right-handed.

When Steve Myers learned that Les Henson's 89-foot-3-inch field goal had been accepted by the "Guinness Book of World Records" as the longest measured basketball shot, he became upset. Myers believes that an extraordinary shot he had made 10 years earlier deserved recognition. However, while Myers' toss was clearly longer than Henson's, the unusual circumstances of the play raised some questions about the validity of his claim. let's examine the stories behind both shots.

Henson's shot occurred with the score tied at 77-77 and the last seconds ticking away. Florida State, the home team, was playing to take the last shot in a televised Metro Conference game with Virginia Tech on January 21, 1980. When State's Parnell Tookes missed his shot from the foul line, Tech's Les Henson grabbed the long rebound halfway between the basket and the corner of the court and heaved the ball toward his own basket. The final buzzer sounded while the ball was in the air. The shot hit the back of the rim and fell through the hoop, winning the game for Virginia Tech 79-77.

Les Henson, a 6-foot-6-inch-tall senior, remembers that he turned to a Florida State cheerleader and asked, "Can you believe that?"

"It was a hope shot, one in a million," he said after the game. "I'll never make a shot like that again."

The first ecstatic news reports of the game claimed the basket was made from 93 feet away. Later, Mark Carlson, Florida State's sports information director, measured the distance, using game films and eye-witnesses' memories to locate the spot from where the shot was taken, and came up with 89 feet 3 inches from Henson's back foot to the back of the rim (where the shot first hit). The game-winning bucket had beaten by 3 inches the previous Guinness record—Rudy Williams'

89-foot toss for Providence College in 1979.

Newspapers around the country picked up the story of Hensen's miracle heave and the major networks secured videotapes of the shot. Radio stations called to interview Les, "The New York Times" spoke with him for an hour, and "Good Morning America" did a special on the play.

Jack Williams, sports information director at Virginia Tech, said that he had never been a part of a single event that had so stirred the country, including a trip to the college nationals during his tenure with the University of North Carolina. Even Les Henson remarked, "All of this commotion over a ball going through a hole."

At the American headquarters for Guinness in New York City, the commotion was just beginning. San Diego resident Steve Myers had contacted Mark Smith of Smith-Ryan Associates, a local public relations firm, to help Myers claim the record he felt was rightfully his. Smith, in turn, called Guinness and explained that his client had made a 95-foot shot 10 years ago.

Guinness' first reaction was complete disbelief. A basketball court, we know, is only 94 feet long! Furthermore, why had this story taken 10 years to surface? Guinness in New York constantly receives exaggerated claims that wither under careful scrutiny, and so this extravagant report was regarded suspiciously. Smith's insistent, high-pressure pitch didn't help, but nonetheless he was invited to send in the written story along with all available documentation. As the eyewitness accounts and news stories dribbled in, it became evident that Steve Myers really had made a most unusual shot. Here's what happened.

At the Pacific Lutheran University gym in Tacoma, Washington, on January 16, 1970, the PLU junior varsity was playing the Cowlitz Redi-Mixers, a local AAU team, in a preliminary game before the regular varsity contest. Witnesses remember that the Redi-Mix team was taking a terrible beating, trailing by over 50 points with 6 minutes left to play. Despite the lopsided score, the PLU team was still applying pressure with a full-court press.

After a PLU basket, Steve Myers prepared to make the in-bounds pass

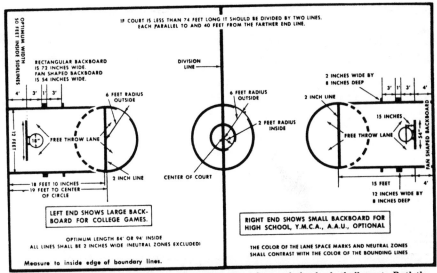

This diagram shows the official layout and dimensions for regulation basketball courts. Both the Florida State and PLU courts are full size at 94 feet long. Many claims for long shots fail to take into account the fact that the backboards are 4 feet in from the endlines.

from behind the endline and to the right of the PLU backboard. Roy Frizzell, Myers' Redi-Mix teammate and now principal of Toutle Lake High School, told Steve to throw him the ball at the other end of the court, hoping to beat the press by passing over it.

Frizzell never got the ball. Myers' pass flew the length of the court and swished through the basket. The

Myers' long shot was made in violation of the rules.

crowd gave Steve a standing ovation and the players from both teams rushed to congratulate him.

Basketball's rules clearly state that a basket does not count if it is made from out-of-bounds. Accordingly, the referees disallowed Myers' bucket. The crowd, already riled by PLU's unsportsmanlike use of a press in the one-sided game, booed the decision. The boos changed to cheers when the referees gave in to

the crowd's sentiment and allowed the 2 points to stand.

Although the original accounts of the game described the shot as a 95-footer, a measurement made in February, 1980, indicated the actual distance was 92 feet 3½ inches. However, it is impossible to accept as exact a measurement made 10 years after the fact. Still, the diagram at the top of the page shows the minimum length such a throw can be.

The PLU court is a regulation 94 feet long inside the endlines. The front of the backboard is 4 feet from the endline and the back of the rim is 6 inches from the backboard. So, the back of the rim is 89 feet 6 inches from the inside of the far endline. Adding the 2-inch width of the boundary line, Myers' shot was at least 89 feet 8 inches long—5 inches longer than Les Henson's. Since Henson's 2-pointer was measured from his back foot, the claim of over 92 feet for Myers' shot is not unreasonable.

So there you have it, all the facts. Myers feels that, since the officials allowed his basket to count, he holds the record. At Guinness, the feeling is that, even though the referees' decision was in the proper spirit of the informal contest, the basket was clearly illegal, tainting Myers' claim, and the play really amounts to an interesting footnote to Les Henson's record. A further consideration is that Henson was aiming for the hoop, while Myers' bucket was, in fact, a wonderful mistake. Oh yes, the Cowlitz Redi-Mix lost the game, 139-52. —Steve Topping ∎

RECORD, RECORD, RECORD —

33 of Them Fell in Basketball When Wilt Chamberlain Centered

Chamberlain's shot sails toward the hoop for one of his 12,681 field goals. Wilt dominates the N.B.A. record book, especially in scoring and rebounding. It was 20 years ago that he scored 100 points in a game, and in later interviews he claimed he could have scored more if the opposition had not tried to keep the ball away from him by fouling his teammates and running out the 24-second clock.

The "Guinness Book of Sports Records, Winners & Champions" does not include a category for the man who holds the most records in sports. But the leading candidate, if there were such a record, would be Wilton Norman Chamberlain, the professional basketball star from 1959 through 1973.

In the Guinness category of National Basketball Association records, Chamberlain's name is listed 33 times. When he left the N.B.A. after 14 seasons, he held 43 major records. Wilt is the only man in the league's history to score 100 points in a game (he had an even 100 playing for the Philadelphia Warriors against the New York Knicks on March 2, 1962), and the closest anyone ever came to that mark was 78—by Chamberlain himself.

His other records include a 50.4 average for the 1961-62 season; 31,419 points for his career; 36 field goals in one game; 28 free throws in one game; 55 rebounds in one game; 59 points in one half; and 18 consecutive field goals made in a game, which he did twice.

Chamberlain's statistics as a scorer are staggering. In the records for one-game performances, he accomplished the following:

Of the eight times that 70 points or more were scored by players in N.B.A. games, Wilt Chamberlain accomplished 6.

Of the 42 times a player scored 60 or more points, Chamberlain was the one who did it 32 times.

Of the 102 times that players scored 55 or more points in a game, Chamberlain did it 73 times.

Chamberlain has 6 of the 7 highest totals for field goals made in a single game.

The contests that matched Wilt Chamberlain (#13) against Bill Russell (#6) provided some of the most exciting moments in N.B.A. history. Chamberlain came away with most of the records, but Russell, as perhaps the most valuable member of the magnificently balanced Boston teams, celebrated 11 N.B.A. championships. Chamberlain only played for two championship teams, but one of them, the 1971-72 Lakers, was the winningest of all time with 69 victories, including 33 in a row.

Though he shot only 54.0 percent on his free throws, he holds the record for the most made (28) in a game, and it took him only 32 shots to make this—the most impressive free-throw shooting night in league history.

In the duels between Chamberlain and the Boston Celtics' Bill Russell that were classics—Chamberlain's offense against Russell's defense—Chamberlain won more often than not. Russell, well known for his rebounding skills, has 8 of the 24 best one-game totals: Chamberlain has 14 of them.

Assists are a category competed in normally by guards, the play-makers of basketball. Tied for 20th place all time for assists in a game was a center, Chamberlain, who had 21 in a

game in 1968, a year when he decided to pass off instead of shooting.

Though he was one of the tallest players in the game, at more than 7 feet (he said 7-1½, others said more like 7-3), he was one of the most durable. In the 1961-62 season, when he was on his biggest scoring binge, Chamberlain played 47 consecutive complete games at one stretch, and 79 complete games in an 80-game season.

As an athlete, Chamberlain was not only versatile on the basketball court, but he was also a superb volleyball player, a fine high jumper and hurdler in track and field, and a man who once considered a pro career as a heavyweight boxer.

Though he was often criticized for not leading his team to win titles—his

teams, namely Philadelphia and Los Angeles, won only two titles, one each during his career—Chamberlain was ready for any challenge.

Perhaps it was in track and field that he proved this most convincingly and then just for a fleeting moment. As a collegian at the University of Kansas, Chamberlain once bet Bill Neider, soon to be the world record holder in the shot put, that he could throw the 16-pound iron ball further than Neider. The bet was made, and Neider proceeded to get off a mighty hefty throw. Then Chamberlain stepped into the circle. Using all his height, weight and agility, he spun with the shot—in a very illegal throw—but he hurled the shot out past Neider's mark, much to the surprise of everyone there, except Chamberlain. ■

JIM JACOBS, WORLD'S GREATEST HANDBALL PLAYER, MODELED HIMSELF AFTER ROBIN, THE BOY WONDER

No, he's not falling over, this is Jim Jacobs' style on the handball court. He gets his entire body behind the shot.

As a boy, Jim Jacobs lived largely in his imagination. Until the age of 15 he was under the spell of comic books. He bought and devoured hundreds of them, and among his heroes were Batman and Robin.

"I always pretended that I was Robin, the Boy Wonder," Jacobs says. "Superman I admired, but Batman and Robin were human, and

everything athletic that Robin did, I tried to do. He threw a boomerang. I learned how to throw a boomerang. Robin was an excellent tumbler, and so I would run off diving boards to practice double flips. Robin knew jujitsu, so I took lessons. In one issue, Robin swam underwater for two minutes. I didn't know if a kid could swim underwater for a minute. So I tried. I learned first that when you

swim underwater you use up oxygen. So then I learned how to hold my breath underwater. Before long I could swim underwater for two minutes. I didn't want to admit that Robin could do something I couldn't do.

"Being Robin, the Boy Wonder, was a tremendous help to me in sports. All of us are susceptible to our emotions when under stress, and when I was younger I would think: What would Robin do? Instead of succumbing to nervous apprehension, I would transform myself into this other character who was emotionally unaffected."

At Los Angeles High School, Jacobs was rarely eligible for sports because of poor grades, especially in English. He looks back upon his academic career with regret, but at the time he simply was not interested. Instead of competing in school work, he played halfback in football, shortstop in baseball and forward in basketball for a branch of the B'nai B'rith, the national Jewish organization. The competition was keen, because any youngster, regardless of religion, could play.

When Jacobs was 19 after he had given up pretending that he was Robin, the Boy Wonder, he began playing four-wall handball at the Hollywood YMCA. Art Linkletter, the TV star, had been playing the sport at the Y for a number of years, and, when Jacobs first started Linkletter had no trouble beating him. But Jacobs was determined to be the best. Naturally right-handed, he spent hours in front of a mirror at home practicing left-hand returns.

Whenever Jacobs passed the May Company department store he would stop for five minutes to check his handball form in the reflection of a large window. "People used to think I was kooky," he says. Within several months, however, he had no trouble thrashing Linkletter or anyone else in Los Angeles. Linkletter and several other enthusiasts, sensing that they had a prodigy in their midst, raised money and sent Jacobs to the junior nationals in Bremerton, Washington, where he won the singles title.

While on a trip to Chicago, Jacobs managed to wangle a singles game against Gus Lewis, the former national champion. After Lewis played Jacobs he called his boss, a multimillionaire named Robert Kendler, and said, "I've just played a kid who doesn't know what he's doing, and for a kid, he's a hell of a handball player."

Kendler immediately hired Jacobs and had him practice at the club with others.

Jacobs spent a year and a half in Chicago, then he was drafted. He served in Japan and Korea and after his discharge he applied himself diligently to handball. In 1953 he

competed in his first nationals and finished fifth. In 1954 he was third, and in 1955, playing on his home court in L.A., he won the singles.

Handball not only requires great speed and an extra quick eye, but muscles that pack power for hitting the ball. Jim Jacobs got these muscles through constant practice, playing three or four games of handball consecutively.

Up until this victory, handball had largely been a power game of kills but Jacobs, having mastered the soft game with ceiling shots, forced his opponents to the rear of the court where they could not make slambang kills. In handball circles Jacobs' play in this match was revolutionary for the sport.

As the "Guinness Book of World Records" says, Jim Jacobs became "the most successful player" in the U.S. Handball Association National Four-Wall Championships.

Jim Jacobs has won six singles titles in the years 1955, '56, '57, '60, '64, and '65—and shared in six doubles titles in 1960, '62, '63, '65, '67 and '68.

Handball is a demanding sport

that requires endurance, speed, power and dexterity, all of which the muscular Jacobs, who now stands 5 feet 9 and weighs 175 pounds, has in abundance. In handball, which has more than five million devotees in the U.S., Jacobs is generally hailed as the finest player of all time. Indeed, there are those who say Jacobs was the best athlete, regardless of sport, in the country.

Once, when Jacobs took a boat to England in search of rare fight films, he signed up for lessons with a steward in the ship's three-wall handball court. He made no mention of his handball experience, and every morning at 10 he presented himself for a hour's instruction. Each day Jacobs permitted his game to improve, and after the last lesson the steward told him, "You're by far the best student I've ever had. For the first time I really feel like a teacher."

To the surprise of most players who hear him for the first time, Jacobs does not dote on techniques, such as how to serve, but on what he calls handball concepts.

"Every player is different physically," Jacobs once told *Sports Illustrated* "so what is good for one man may be bad for another. Instead of trying to change their swings or serves, I tell them when to go on offense and when to go on defense. There are certain basic rules, and if you violate them and your opponent does not, you simply cannot win. For example, never return the ball to the front wall first unless you intend to end the volley on that particular shot, because the ball gets back to the server too quickly. Also, whenever possible, take the ball out of the air to keep your opponent in the backcourt. The man closest to the front wall is the man on the offense. I believe I'm effective because my opponents can't get me out of the front of the court.

"Another concept in handball is to make your opponent hit every ball with his weak arm. If your right hand is your strong arm, it's your right hand that wins games and the left that loses them. Unfortunately, many young players have developed their weak arm to the point where it looks as good as their stronger arm, and if the ball is just a fraction to the left of the middle of the court, they'll hit it with their left arm. In the beginning they might do all right but, after playing an hour or two, the

LeRoy Neiman, in this painting, captures Jim Jacobs' tremendous power and agility.

basic weakness of the arm begins to show. But there are players who will continue to play with both hands just to get the ooh and ahs.

"I'm supposed to have arms of equal strength, but I really look upon my right hand, my strong hand, as the sword and the left as the shield. I tell players that when they have a comfortable, convenient choice to use their stronger arm."

Away from handball, Jacobs has achieved a certain amount of standing as a collector of comic books and fight films. He has the largest collections of both kinds in the world, and both have fitted into his sporting endeavors.

As a youngster in L.A., Jacobs had always been fascinated by boxing, and when he was 14 he bought his first film of a fight, the first Louis-Walcott bout, to find out who really won. After giving the decision to Walcott, Jacobs began acquiring

films of other fights. He bought and traded films with collectors and museums around the world. Many films had never been seen before; they had lain in pictorial limbo for years because federal law from 1912 to 1940 prohibited the interstate shipment of fight films. The law had been passed as a result of the race riots that took place all over the country after Jack Johnson beat Jim Jeffries.

In addition to obtaining films, Jacobs also began acquiring the legal rights to show them for exhibition purposes.

In 1959, a collector in Australia wrote Jacobs that he had a copy of the Johnson-Willard fight film. No other copy was known, and the price was $5,000. Jacobs got in touch with Bill Cayton in New York, who was the producer of a television series, "Greatest Fights of the Century" and Cayton agreed to advance the

money. Jacobs flew to Australia, inspected the film and bought it. He took it to New York where he agreed to pool his collection with Cayton's and go into business with him.

Jacobs and Cayton are also the managers of boxer Wilfredo Benitez. When Benitez won the WBC super-lightweight championship at the age of 17, he was the youngest fighter ever to win a world championship. He now holds three titles: welterweight (WBC), junior welterweight (WBA), and light middleweight (WBC).

"Sugar Ray Robinson," said Jim Jacobs, "was the greatest fighter of his time—in fact, of all time, and he got $160,000—$175,000 tops. In a recent fight, Roberto Duran and Sugar Ray Leonard got a total of $15,000,000. If Sugar Ray Robinson were fighting today, the money he could earn would equal the national debt." ∎

FASTEST RUNNING WAITER

Roger Bourban, Swiss Californian, does wonders running a marathon carrying open bottle on a tray

by David Spetner

Have you ever tried walking down a long hall with a small tray in one hand and an open bottle on the tray? How about running in a race 26 miles 385 yards long in 3 hours 6 minutes, without spilling a drop out of the bottle and without shifting the tray to the other hand?

You say no one can do this? Well, Roger Bourban can—and did it in the London marathon in March 1981. Moreover, Roger has run in many marathons. However, Roger's time in the London race was his fastest up to that time, a feat that is recognized in the 1982 Guinness Book.

(Since then, Roger has beaten his own time, with a record marathon run of 2 hours 55 minutes in the Nike Race in Eugene, Oregon, on September 13, 1981.)

"The greatest degree of competition is not for *me* to compete against *you*, nor you against me, but for each of us to reach within the depths of our capabilities and to perform to the greatest of our potential." So stated Roger Bourban as he relaxed for a moment at a table in his Beverly Hills restaurant.

Roger did not always dream of setting a Guinness record. He grew up in the small town of Sion, Switzerland where he was born on May 10, 1948. His parents owned a French restaurant and Roger and his two sisters and one brother lived in an apartment above. The Swiss are generally athletic people and Roger was no exception as he excelled in skiing and became a member of the regional Swiss team until a bad accident dampened his plans to rise in that sport. From skiing he took up judo and before long made the national team, but it was never Roger's intention to go professional. As a youngster, his parents put him to work at his first love, the family restaurant, and, early on, Roger showed great promise as a chef's apprentice. In 1965, Roger applied to and was accepted to the Ecole Hoteliere of Lausanne, one of the most prestigious hotel and restaurant schools in the world, and it was there that he became a master chef.

Swiss-born Roger Bourban is not only a running waiter he is also a European-trained master chef.

Talk of travel abounds in Swiss restaurants as most of the clientele are tourists, visiting for a chance to sample some of the best food in the world. The constant talk of adventure convinced Roger to leave his native country to find out for himself what lay beyond the Swiss Alps. After living in England for a year, Roger moved to Australia to work as the manager of the El Camino in Sydney. At the time, he continued to train hard in judo and in 1971 won the Sydney Cup. But even at age 23, Roger had still not begun running as a serious sport.

In 1972, Roger came to San Diego, California, and fell in love with America. Before long he found himself in great demand in some of the better French restaurants in Beverly Hills and worked as a chef, captain or waiter.

In 1976, the first Los Angeles International Waiter's Race was held, including a course of only 250 yards where all runners were required to carry a tray with a bottle. Roger won the race and was astounded by the excitement he created. Not only was Roger enthusiastic about this new found sport, the city of Beverly Hills decided to sponsor its own race and expanded the waiter's race to three divisions including courses of 1, 5, and 10 kilometers. Not only did Roger Bourban win each division, he was the only waiter to finish the 10 kilometer that first year.

Although he did run in the 1978 L.A. Waiter's Race, Roger did manage to run and win the next three annual races and the next four Beverly Hills races, continuing to set new records each time out.

In 1979, one of the race sponsors, Perrier, asked Roger to run in the October New York City Marathon. That encouragement was all Roger needed and over the next several months, he ran nearly 2,000 miles, sometimes carrying bricks in each hand as he set out to carry his tray and a bottle of Perrier water through the five boroughs of the Big Apple. Roger finished that first marathon in New York in 3 hours 21 minutes, which won him his first mention in the Guinness Book.

In 1980, Roger fulfilled another major goal—he became a U.S. citizen. He also opened his own French restaurant in Beverly Hills, the Café Monet Bistro.

Roger has never given up his fondness for the kitchen and he continues to rise each dawn to bake his fruit tarts, the specialty of his restaurant. Between his earlier races in 1976, Roger, acting on a bet celebrating the U.S. bicentennial, baked 201 tarts (9½″ diameters each) to honor America at the Waldorf Astoria Hotel in New York. He accomplished the feat in 11 hours 55 minutes and before collapsing from exhaustion, baked a special peanut tart to honor Jimmy Carter.

If you can catch up to Roger, you'll find him a likeable, hardworking, disciplined achiever. ■

JESSE OWENS

AMERICA'S MAN ON THE RUN WAS EVEN GREATER THAN GUINNESS RECORDS SHOW

For almost 50 years J.C. "Jesse" Owens was America's man on the run. He sprinted to national fame in high school in Cleveland, Ohio, later at Ohio State University, and in 1935 and 1936 set records that were truly amazing.

Owens enjoyed promoting the things he believed in—sport in general, the Olympics, his country, his black race. With an engaging smile and velvet voice, he did his job well. Universally accepted as the first great popular black athlete in America, Owens was a step ahead of boxer Joe Louis, and some major companies were quick to utilize his ability to promote.

Yet there may have been one area where he came up short in promoting, and that was his own records. For all of Owens' greatness— the high school records, the college records, world records, Olympic gold medals and Olympic records— Owens was probably even greater than history gave him credit for.

And certainly, Owens has enough credits in the record books.

In the 1936 Olympics, he won four gold medals—in the 100- and 200-meter dashes, the long jump and the 400-meter relay. No one else had ever won that many in a single Olympics.

In National Collegiate Athletic Association competition, he won eight first places in eight events, something no athlete in N.C.A.A. history has come close to matching.

In a 45-minute span at the 1935 Big Ten Conference meet, he set three world records and tied another.

Yet in each instance, his marks were probably even better than their face value. Owens ran in an era when tracks were covered with cinder, not the bouncy synthetic and near-flawless surfaces that are used today. There were no starting blocks for a firm start; Owens and other runners of his day had to dig holes in the cinders in order to get a firm footing at the starting line.

When Owens was promoting the 3M Company's synthetic tracks in the 1960's he was asked to analyze what he could have done on such surfaces. In not a bragging way, he said, "I may have done a 9.2 in the 100. And with a rubberized runway, I probably would have broad jumped over 27 feet, maybe even 28." It was a rare moment for Owens, who would have preferred to tell people that

Proud of his four gold medals won in the Olympics, Jesse Owens won many honors besides, starting in high school in Cleveland and at Ohio State University.

Jesse Owens never had starting blocks when he set world records in 1935 and 1936.

young athletes of the generations that followed him were faster, stronger, and probably better than he was.

Owens competed in four events at the Berlin Olympics in 1936, when he was 22. Nowadays, few American sprinters compete in more than one Olympic individual event, plus a relay. Only two men from any nation have won both the 100 and the 200 since 1936. Yet despite a heavy schedule in 1936, when he ran eight races (prelims, semifinals, finals) in four days, then two relay races three days later, plus the long jump—Owens set Olympic records that have stood the test of time.

His long jump record lasted for 24 years. His 100-meter record in the Olympics was tied often, but not broken until 1960. His 200-meter time at the 1936 Olympics was not bettered until 1956.

Nobody has come close to winning eight first places in eight attempts in the N.C.A.A. meet. Yet Owens did it in only two years. He was not eligible as a freshman in 1934, as freshmen are today, yet he was the best sprinter in America then. And he decided to forego his senior year of college in 1937 and turned professional because he wanted to make money for his family.

But for all his many remarkable achievements, his greatest performance—namely setting four world records within 45 minutes on May 25, 1935 (six records actually, as his two 220-yard events were also ratified as records for the equivalent 200 meters)—was vastly underrated, too, if that can be believed.

On that day, at the University of Michigan's track in Ann Arbor, Owens' conditions were hardly made for world records.

For one thing, he had been suffering from a back injury as the result of a fraternity rough-housing session back in Columbus, Ohio.

Yet he started out the meet with a world record-tying 9.4 seconds in the 100-yard dash. (It was not his first 9.4 either; he once did it in high school, but was not given credit for a world record.)

The man who was the head timer that day, Phil Diamond, recalled at the time of Owens' death at the age of 66 in 1980, that the clocking, though accurate, is somewhat misleading. He said: "Each of the four timers caught Owens just a mere shade over 9.3 seconds, but we had to give him credit for 9.4. He would've beaten a 9.4 man by almost a yard."

Furthermore, Diamond's team insisted that a runner must cover a full distance, that his torso must cross the finish line, not just touch the imaginary line that is indicated by the finishing tape. That could mean another fraction of a second, and probably enough to get Owens' time down to a clear 9.3.

In the 220-yard dash (which is about a meter longer than a 200-meter run), Owens ran a 20.3 on the straightaway. Though he was ahead of the field by about 8 yards after 150 yards of the race, Owens turned on the speed for some reason. His coach at the time, Larry Snyder, said he watched Owens "turn it on" for the only time ever. But Owens was concerned about back muscle tension. Other than that day, according to Snyder, Owens never ran for records.

The long jump had been scheduled that day between the 100 and the 220 races and was not expected to finish until after the later race. This was a disadvantage to a multi-event athlete such as Owens. Another disadvantage: to spur the interest of the 9,000 fans at Michigan's Ferry Field, a new long-jump runway had been laid out on the grass, nearer the stands, instead of on the traditional cinders, which were faster for the runners.

Owens' competition included a man who could do well over 25 feet, so the Ohio State star decided to put his best effort into his first jump—then rush back for the 220-yard competition. Owens put a handkerchief in the pit at 26 feet 2½ inches, Diamond recalled. That happened to be the world record. "When I saw him do that," Diamond recalled, "I thought, 'boy, is he a cocky kid.'"

Owens cleared the hanky for a world-record 26 feet 8¼ inches on the first and only try.

In the other event in which he set a world record that day, the 220-yard hurdles (an event that was later discontinued in the 1960's), Owens demolished the opposition. The world record was 23 seconds. Owens was hardly a polished hurdler, being a short man who had to struggle with form. But he could combine his jumping ability with his sprint talent to make up for his lack of technique. Owens ran a 22.6. Diamond recalled: "He was caught at 22.4, 22.5, and 22.6." Nowadays the middle time would be accepted.

One can only wonder if Owens had been in perfect physical shape that afternoon, if he had had the benefit of starting blocks and modern runways, if the timers timed as they do today, and if Owens had been able to concentrate on just one or two events, what records he might have established. ∎

THE WIZARD OF ICE

BOBBY ORR REVEALS ALL IN EXCLUSIVE INTERVIEW

Hockey Fans Demand Good Skating, Puck Control Fed Up with Long Delays & Foolishness

Who is the greatest ice hockey player of all time? Walk down any main street in Canada asking that question and you're sure to start an argument. There are some certainties, though. Only a few players will be nominated for the honor, and one of the nominees will be Bobby Orr—pride of the Boston Bruins, the NHL's all-time top-scoring defenseman, Guinness recordholder with six consecutive 100-point seasons, and the recipient of more individual honors and awards than any other player in NHL history.

Guinness reporter Geri Martin visited Bobby Orr in his home near Boston, Massachusetts, where he lives with his wife, Margaret, and his two sons, Darren and Brent.

"I was struck by how natural and unaffected Bobby is," Geri reported. "He's so easy-going, I would forget that I was with one of sports' greatest superstars. While we were sitting together in a restaurant, for example, it became obvious that 90 percent of the diners were aware that Bobby Orr was in the room, but he seemed completely undisturbed by it."

Bobby Orr revolutionized play at his position, racking up goals and assists with a speed unprecedented among defensemen. He was an excellent skater—fast and fluid, with great acceleration and the ability to change direction quickly. Orr shot the puck with great accuracy. His hard, left-handed slap shot exploded at the goalie and, from in close, his wrist shot found the unguarded corners of the net with amazing frequency. Bobby Orr used these talents

Guinness reporter Geri Martin gets exclusive interview with Bobby Orr in Boston.

to blaze a trail that other scoring-minded defensemen have followed.

By no means did Orr neglect his defensive responsibilities. For each player, teams in the NHL keep an interesting statistic called "plus-minus." This statistic measures the difference between goals scored by and against a team while a player is on the ice. During his career, Bobby Orr's tally was 1,188 by his team, and 591 against, a difference of plus 597—which the official NHL Guide described as "amazing for a defenseman."

Born on March 20, 1948, in Parry Sound, Ontario, Robert Gordon Orr was skating by the time he was three. At age 14, Bobby started playing junior hockey for the Oshawa Generals, an arrangement involving a 115-mile commute, and he was soon known as the best schoolboy player in Canada.

Orr joined the Boston Bruins when he was 18 years old, and played his first regular-season game on October

19, 1966. That night, wearing sweater number 4, he collected the first of his many assists. Before he retired, Bobby Orr more than doubled the regular-season records for goals, assists and points by a defenseman. Indeed, his 102 assists in 1970-71 stood as the all-league mark until 1980-81. Orr set an NHL record by scoring 100 or more points in six consecutive seasons.

When Bobby Orr broke the old career marks for goals, assists and points by a defenseman, he accomplished it in far fewer games than the previous recordholders.

During his 13-year career, Orr underwent six operations on his left knee, but the knee would not respond to the surgery and Bobby had to retire much earlier than he would have wished.

It was a sad day for hockey when, on November 8, 1978, Bobby Orr officially announced that his playing days were over. Although he had hung up his skates, several honors still awaited Bobby. In a moving tribute to him, Orr's sweater number 4 was officially retired during a ceremony at Boston Garden before an exhibition game between the Bruins and Soviet Wings on January 9, 1979. On September 12, 1979, Bobby Orr was inducted into the Hockey Hall of Fame, the youngest person ever to receive the honor.

GUINNESS: *When you were growing up, were there certain coaches or individuals or set of circumstances that helped you become such a great all-around player?*
BOBBY ORR: When I was growing up, we were coached by a local group

24

Although remembered as a scorer, Orr did not neglect his defenseman's responsibility. When Bobby was on the ice with the teams at even strength, his team outscored its opponents two-to-one. Here he stands ready to help goalie Gilles Gilbert.

of men who were not ex-hockey players or anything like that, didn't play professional hockey or junior hockey, but were simply interested in the kids. The two main things they stressed were: you're supposed to have fun playing amateur sports, and learn the fundamentals of the game.

My parents were certainly a great influence on me. I can't ever remember my parents forcing me to play or saying, "Hey, we want you to be a professional player," or anything like that. They'd buy my equipment, they drove me to the games and to practices, and so on. My parents are the big reason I became a professional hockey player.

I love to play, I enjoy playing, I love the practice and it's a great position to be in when you love doing something, enjoy working at it, enjoy practicing and get paid the way we get paid—and after I became a professional, I got paid very well.

G: *With your great skating ability,* *why did you choose to be a defenseman?*

BOBBY ORR: I really started out as a right winger, and a gentleman by the name of Bucko Macdonald—I guess I would have been a squirt then about 9 or 10 years old—tried me out at defense and I liked it. I didn't play the position the way you're supposed to play it. I was known as an offensive defenseman and many times an offensive defenseman gives the coach gray hairs, but the fellows I played with backed me up many, many times and really bailed me out of a lot of trouble.

G: *No NHL defenseman had ever accumulated as many goals and assists as you, and now many more defensemen look to score. What is the main responsibility of a defenseman on the ice? What did you do to change, or add to that?*

BOBBY ORR: The main responsibility of a defenseman is to defend when the other team is on the offense.

When the puck is in his end, it's his job to get in the corners and try to get the puck out to the forwards. He also watches front of the net.

As I said earlier, I did not play defense like you're supposed to. I carried the puck a lot. Some defensemen do it—more today than a few years back—but when you're an offensive defenseman, it's important that your teammates know your style. If you should carry the puck up the ice, it's important that one of the forwards drop back to take your position to back you up. On teams I played with, the players knew my style and, as I said earlier, they bailed me out of a lot of trouble.

G: *What difficulties did you have breaking into the NHL?*

BOBBY ORR: I was very, very fortunate breaking into the NHL. The Boston Bruins were a heck of a bunch of guys. There was a lot written about me before I went to camp and the players could have made it very difficult for me, but they didn't. They took me under their wings. I was a little bit shy and afraid of going out with them to dinner, and they insisted that I do go, so they made it a lot easier on this young hotshot rookie who was coming to camp.

The big difference when I broke into the NHL was that everyone was a good player. In junior hockey and minor hockey most teams had a few good players, but in the NHL every player was a good player. Their styles were different, but you were defending all the time against the good player and the thing you had to realize was that everyone was dangerous and you had to be on your toes all the time.

G: *Many fans, and some players as well, feel that NHL play has grown unnecessarily rough, including too much fighting. Do you agree with that point of view?*

BOBBY ORR: I believe that hockey is a contact game, it's a tough game, but I think there's far too much foolishness, although it's been reduced the last few years. Still, I think there's far too much foolishness—the bench clearings, the long delays, the players using their sticks in ways they shouldn't—I think there's still a little bit too much of that.

The contact will always be in the game. Hockey is a contact sport and the good hip check, for example, is part of the game. It should be there and I'm sure will always be there, but

Bobby Orr, the NHL's all-time highest-scoring defenseman, racked up 270 goals and 645 assists for 915 points in 657 regular-season games. His career average of 1.393 points per game is the league record for players at any position with a minimum of 500 lifetime points.

the bench clearings. A lot of people use the word violence—I don't even call it violence, I call it foolishness. It's been reduced, but the league must continue making rule changes, as they're doing now, to try to curb it. They're making the rules stricter, the fines are heavier, and so on. I believe they must continue to get this foolishness out of the game.

I believe the fan today wants to see good contact, puck control and good skating. They're fed up with long delays and the foolishness that has been going on.

G: *Many Canadian youngsters grow up dreaming of winning the Stanley Cup—and you scored two Cup-winning goals! Was it as great a thrill as you expected?*

BOBBY ORR: I was fortunate enough to score two winning goals in the Stanley Cup final play. Whether I had scored those goals or not, we did win and being on Stanley Cup winning teams was just as great a thrill as I thought it might be. But, it would have been just as thrilling whether I had scored the goals or not. Yes, it was certainly a great, great thrill.

G: *It takes more than a few outstanding players to win the Stanley Cup, it* takes a strong, all-around team. *What made those Cup-winning Bruin teams so good? If you were putting a team together, what would you look for and what kind of play would you stress?*

BOBBY ORR: If you look around at the good teams, there's a mixture of everything: the offensive player, the defensive player, your specialists, your penalty-killers, and, of course, good goaltending. In order to have a winning combination, you've got to have a mix of everything.

If you go back to the winning Bruin teams, we were a close group and I think that's one of the things that made us successful those few years. Everything wasn't hunky-dory all the time off the ice, but when that puck was dropped everyone did his job and that made us successful.

If I were putting a team together today, I would look for that mix. You can't have all offense, or you're going to get killed on defense. You're going to have your specialists and goaltending.

In the way that the game is going now, if you're not a good skating club you're not going to win many hockey games in the NHL today.

G: *What are some of the outstanding moments, beside Stanley Cup play, that you remember from your career?*

BOBBY ORR: I can still remember my first game in 1966—how nervous I was, getting to the rink at 1 o'clock in the afternoon for a night game, and I can still remember the game. Of course, the Stanley Cup winning teams are great memories—the parade down Washington Street, the Boston City Hall reception.

I think in 1967 finally getting a chance to play for Canada in the Canada Cup and being on the winning team. Playing against the Europeans was a great thrill.

G: *When you were playing, which forwards were the most difficult for you to defend against, and which goalies were the toughest to score on?*

BOBBY ORR: The forwards were all difficult. If you don't play them properly they're going to beat you.

A guy like Bobby Hull was so fast he could go outside you and beat you with his speed and his strength. He could shoot from center ice, and the way he shot the puck he could *score* from center ice.

Then you'd run into guys like (Stan) Mikita—he was so good with the puck. Not only did you have to watch him—he could go right through you to the net—but you had to look around because he passed the puck so blasted well, you knew someone would be coming late. So, you'd be watching him, but you'd also have to be watching the late guy because of the way Stan passed the puck. He was just so shrewd.

Then you'd get the speed of an Yvan Courneyer. The players were all different, some in the way they shot, their strength—you had to defend against them differently. I just mentioned three or four, but they were all tough—especially if you didn't play them right they would beat you and possibly score.

Goalies: I think Tony Esposito is still one of the top goaltenders in the league, and was when I was playing.

G: *How does the European (or Soviet) style of hockey compare to the NHL's? Is the NHL picking up some of that style?*

BOBBY ORR: The big thing we've picked up from the Europeans or Soviet teams is puck control. I don't think today we shoot the puck in and forecheck as much as we used to. We still do a lot of forechecking, but we control that puck now. What they've learned from us is how to forecheck, and the contact part of the game. I can remember the first time around, they did very little forechecking.

G: *Were the NHL players surprised to find the Russian teams were so good?*

BOBBY ORR: Before we played against the Soviets, we didn't think they were going to be as good as they were—as good as they *are.* They're a good hockey team, a solid hockey team, and after the first series I think we all woke up and said, "Hey, they were a heck of a lot better than we thought they'd be."

G: *You would probably still be playing if it weren't for your unfortunate knee injuries. What was the problem, exactly?*

BOBBY ORR: I had a lot of cartilage problems. The joint in my left knee closed up so I've got a lot of bone on bone, and a lot of chipping in the joints. The chips get caught and cause my knee to lock or give out on me.

G: *What are you doing now? Are you still involved with ice hockey?*

BOBBY ORR: Today I spend most of my time with Nabisco Brands, Inc. I do a lot of work with youngsters—clinics and different programs for kids. I just finished a film on youth sports for Nabisco Brands. We put this film together because we feel that there's too much emphasis on winning at all costs. Playing should be fun but a lot of the time it isn't.

In the film I point out that to coach kids, you only have to stress the fundamentals—skating, puck control and passing. Kids watch the pros play and try to copy what they see. The NHL must set a firm example. When fighting occurs, the players should be made to pay stiffer fines—and out of their own pockets, not the team's till. We who love hockey have to change the way things are today. Just a couple of interested people are not enough. I'm going to keep fighting.

G: *What can you tell youngsters who might wish to become professional hockey players, or pro athletes in any sport? How can they prepare? What can they expect?*

BOBBY ORR: If you look around the league, there are very few players who can't skate. There are smooth skaters and there are rough skaters, but they all got there. So, if you plan on being a professional hockey player, skating is very important.

The old saying, good things don't come easy, holds true, and whether it be hockey or another professional sport, you have to work at it. I don't care how much ability you're blessed with, if you don't work at your sport, then you're not going to be successful, you're not going to make it.

What can they expect? If you plan on being a professional in any sport, you can expect a tough road, but once you're there, being a professional athlete is a great life. I wouldn't have wanted to trade it for anything.

■

Bobby Orr believes in starting young to learn the fundamentals of hockey—skating especially. Be a good skater first, have fun skating and playing, and don't put too much emphasis on winning is what he tells youngsters.

BICYCLING CHAMPION MARINO REVEALS HOW HE TRAINED FOR TRANS-AMERICA RECORD

John Marino, a 32-year-old physical education instructor from Newport Beach, California, pedaled over 2,861 miles in only 12 days 3 hours 41 minutes to set a Guinness record for trans-America cycling from Santa Monica, California, to New York City, bettering 21 hours and 39 minutes, the previous record he had set in 1978.

In those twelve days of riding, Marino averaged nearly 240 miles per day on his Peugeot PY10. Cycling through 116-degree desert heat, 7,900-foot Rocky Mountain passes, and hot, humid midwestern plains, he slept not more than 4½ hours per day, often less.

This extraordinary feat of strength and endurance burned a comparable number of calories, according to Dr. Lawrence May of UCLA Medical School, to swimming the English Channel 18 times or playing both offense and defense in 256 Super Bowls. Yet, only six years ago John Marino was an overweight, self-described "junk food junkie" who had not exercised in five years because of a chronic back ailment.

John Marino cycled through all kinds of terrain—deserts, mountains, plains, and city streets during his successful assault on the transcontinental record.

Marino logged 100 miles a day to train for his 1980 record journey. This "stress cycling" was designed to build up his heart and lungs. He had trained for 3 years before his first record ride in 1978.

Marino began bicycling as a way to exercise without hurting his back. Before long he was able to pedal 100 miles per day although his injury, from which doctors had said he would never recover, still does not permit him to run.

As his body became stronger through exercise, Marino developed an interest in nutrition, discovering that different foods affected him in different ways. His first dietary change was to stop eating meat. Now he eats only organically grown foods: fruits, vegetables, grains, and herbs.

Nutrition has become Marino's major concern. In 1978, when he set his first coast-to-coast record of 13 days 80 minutes, Marino attributed 50 percent of his success to diet.

"You are what you eat," Marino said. "Diet is the fuel-mix that determines the efficiency of body and mind functions."

Having experimented with several controversial nutrition programs over the years, he finds that a low-protein, high-carbohydrate diet works best.

John Marino's totally unorthodox approach to fitness includes cytotoxic medicine, regular "cleansing" (fasting and enemas), deep-tissue therapy, mind-over-matter psychology, high negative low instake, and plenty of exercise.

Cytotoxic medicine is based on the theory that all people have an allergic reaction to different foods, and it is possible to determine through tests which foods are beneficial to an individual and which foods are not. This system also stresses that even beneficial foods can cause a negative reaction if they are eaten too often, so foods must be rotated for an efficient diet.

Marino and his health advisors believe, nevertheless, that toxins inevitably accumulate in the human body. He flushes these toxins out with a weekly fast that is combined with other purgative measures. Deep-tissue massage also rids the body of poisons. Unlike Swedish massage, which concentrates on various muscle groups, deep-tissue therapy cleanses the body by actually breaking down the toxic deposits which tend to crystallize in lymph glands, nerve endings, and capillary areas.

Negative ions were supplied by a generator in the motor home that accompanied Marino on his journey. The devise emits negatively charged electrons which attach themselves to molecules of oxygen, creating ionized oxygen. This improves the body's ability to absorb oxygen and enhances one's sense of well-being. The effect is like "breathing the air after a thunderstorm."

Regular muscle conditioning was a significant aspect of Marino's training program. To build both his leg strength and upper body resiliency, Marino used the popular Nautilus machine, which provides constant muscle tension over the full range of exercise motion, thus enabling him to train more efficiently. Upper body strength is important because arms, shoulders, and hands must absorb constant road shocks which are transmitted up through the bicycle's handlebars.

Just as important was Marino's roadwork. After years of experimentation, he found 100 miles a day of "stress" cycling to be the optimum level. Stress cycling, or riding shorter distances at greater speeds, made training rides of a full 250 miles per day unnecessary. For Marino, practice runs of 100 miles at 22 mph were ideal preparation for riding 250 miles at 15 to 18 mph, the pace he planned for the race.

Arms raised in triumph, Marino pedals the last mile through New York City to City Hall, his final destination, where he arrived at 10:41 a.m. EDT on June 28, 1980. *(AP)*

Although Marino, alone, had to endure the pain, his effort could never have been successful without help. His support crew accompanied him in a motor home, and consisted of a race director, navigator, deep-tissue massage specialist, Cycles Peugeot bike mechanic, cook/housekeeper, and nurse. He was further assisted by an electronic "support crew" that included a mini-computer, an elaborate telecommunications system, and portable electronic medical apparatus. These machines provided such services as monitoring Marino's performance to determine when he was ahead or behind schedule, compiling county-by-county weather and traffic reports to anticipate problems ahead, and checking Marino's medical condition—even relaying information back and forth between the mobile home and a medical lab in

Manhattan Beach, California, where dietary adjustments were suggested.

Marino's training and planning paid off. By the fifth day of his trip he was 24 hours ahead of his 1978 record pace. Marino had tried and failed to break his record in 1979. That attempt had been plagued by an ankle injury, horrible weather, and a poorly chosen northern route through Pennsylvania for the last leg of the journey. Exhausted, Marino had abandoned the attempt only 60 miles from New York City with no hope of arriving on time. To counteract these problems, the 1980 challenge was planned for earlier in the summer when there was less heat and, luckily, less rain. The southern route through Pennsylvania's mountains, used in 1978, was re-adopted.

After just six days—the halfway

point—Marino was still a full day ahead of his 1978 pace. Except for the inevitable heat and sandstorms in the desert, the weather had been splendid. It had not rained, and the fourth, fifth, and sixth days were blessed with overcast skies and cool temperatures, enabling Marino to gobble up the miles. With everything running so smoothly, it was hard to imagine that trouble was just up the road.

The seventh day—Sunday, June 22—proved to be a disaster. First, Marino was soaked by a pelting rain shower. Later, in Ottawa, Kansas, just 45 miles southwest of Kansas City, Missouri, a state trooper blocked Marino's access to route I-35. The trooper offered Marino the choice of taking a hilly 14.3-mile detour or the Interstate. If he chose the Interstate, the trooper warned, it would have meant 36 hours in jail. Ruffled by the unexpected delay and tired by the exhausting detour, Marino was mentally down for the first time during the journey. It was the only day he failed to log at least 200 miles.

Hot, humid weather, trucks, increasing traffic, and the cumulative effects of his strenuous pace, were Marino's obstacles during his four days through the Midwest. By the eleventh day, his feet were sore and blistered, his knees throbbed, and he seemed barely able to sit on his bike. Deep-tissue massage and increased carbohydrates helped to revive him, but mostly John Marino persevered through inner strength.

On June 27, Marino began a nonstop, 317-mile blitz from Roxbury, Pennsylvania, to New York City. Attacking the Blue Ridge Mountains, whose grades are frequently steeper than the Rockies', Marino kept up an extraordinary 12-to-13-mph pace uphill. Pedaling through the night and into the next morning, Marino crossed New Jersey to the Holland Tunnel and entered New York City, where he rode triumphantly to City Hall and into record fame.

Realizing that many people might find his health program too austere, John Marino nonetheless recommends it to the general public. However, he cautions everyone to train gradually. "Overdoing it—pushing your body too hard, too fast—is the greatest danger to health." It's hard to argue with a man who had gone from an overweight semi-invalid to a world record holder in six strenuous years. ∎

PELÉ,
THE SOCCER STAR
AMERICA LOVES

Pelé was not the first soccer star in America but he was the one who popularized professional soccer with his skill and charisma, even though he played in only 90 games in the U.S. in the twilight of his career. He set a world record by scoring 1,216 goals in 1,254 games for his Brazilian team, Santos, 1956-1974.

To millions of Americans, soccer had a reserved seat on the same plane that brought Pelé winging out of Brazil. The vast majority, sports fans or otherwise, had never seen a soccer ball, let alone a game, before Pelé arrived on American shores, but that's hardly to say it hadn't been here. Yes, soccer had been around for quite a while, but it existed in the shadow of numerous other sports and leisure-time activities. Professional soccer had been struggling for the public's attention and, then in 1975, Pelé's $4,500,000 contract captured it.

Pelé was not the beginning of American soccer, as many people assume; instead he provided an extraordinary shot in the arm that put this rapidly growing game onto the front page and into the public eye. He played 90 games with the New York Cosmos of the North American Soccer League, and it was his presence that gave credibility to American professional soccer, both in the media and in the world soccer community.

European critics had consistently looked upon American professional soccer as a collection of has-beens along with never-weres, but Pelé's undeniable skill and charisma, even in the twilight of his lengthy career, brought new attention from the toughest critics. Pelé's presence also focused attention on the booming growth of youth soccer and the obvious skill that was coming from those ranks. Soccer is one major sport where physical size is not of prime importance and any youngster can play. In fact, it was the soccer youth of America who really took Pelé to their heart and he returned their devotion by demanding that the media turn its attention to them. ■

QUEER GOINGS-ON IN THE MINOR LEAGUES

Baseball Strike Focused Attention on Farm Clubs and Some World Records

In the mid-summer of 1981, when major league baseball players went on strike for 50 days, Americans became starved enough for baseball action that they turned to the source their parents and grandparents turned to before the advent of television—minor league ball. For the minors, it meant a popularity unmatched since the post-World War II 1940's, when the minors burgeoned with teams and players across the United States, Canada and Mexico. During the 1981 strike, for instance, minor league teams were invited to fill the gap and play in major league stadiums. Some huge crowds came out. Television, and even some radio stations, in the major league cities began to carry the minor league games of teams that had agreements with those cities' major league teams.

And one night in Pawtucket, Rhode Island, 54 newspapers and three television networks covered an unusual game—which, because of the gap left by the striking big-leaguers, became the biggest story for some sports pages the next day.

The Pawtucket Red Sox and the Rochester (New York) Red Wings had played 32 innings on the night of April 18 and well into the next morning. At 4:07 a.m. on April 19, 8 hours and 7 minutes after the game began, the contest was suspended, and rescheduled to resume June 23.

The 32 innings constituted a record for a professional game, three more innings than that played by Miami and St. Petersburg in a 1966 Florida State League game.

Because the major leaguers were still playing in April, the first segment of the Pawtucket-Rochester game got very little publicity. Instead of 54 newspaper reporters on hand, there were only 19 fans left in the stands when the game was suspended. But with the minors in the spotlight in June, 5,756 fans showed up, unusually large for a minor league contest.

What they saw in June was a quick ending to baseball's longest game.

Back in the April segment of the game, a total of 36 players went to bat a total of 213 times. But in the top of the 33rd inning in June, Bob Ojeda, ace of the Pawtucket Red Sox staff, gave up only a single in putting the Red Wings out. Ojeda's teammates went to bat, quickly loaded the bases and scored the winning run before an out was made. After 8 hours 25 minutes on the field, 67 days apart, the game was over.

Some strange statistics, reflected in the accompanying box score (right) emerged from the game. But baseball fans learned all over again that the minor leagues have some strange records to offer to baseball lore. That was nothing new.

In 1978, the Society for American Baseball Research, a group of amateur statisticians and historians who take a professional approach to their hobby, compiled a book called "Minor League Baseball Stars." In an introductory chapter, the comment was made:

"Some truly remarkable records were established in the lower classifications. In fact, every significant season record made in the majors was bettered in the minors, except for three-base hits."

The *Guinness Book of Sports Records, Winners and Champions* lists some of those significant marks, including the 72 home runs by Joe Bauman, of the Rosewell, New Mexico team, in 1954 (the major league record is 61, held by Roger Maris, New York Yankees, 1961); the most home runs in a game, 8, by Justin Clarke of the Corsicana, Texas, team, 1902 (the most hit in a major league game is 4, held by several players); and the longest home run, 618 feet, by Dizzy Carlyle, at Emeryville, California, in 1929.

The longest measured throw, 445 feet 10 inches, was by minor leaguer Glen Gorbous, in 1957, and the fastest man to circle the bases under a stop watch was Ernest Evar Swanson, another minor leaguer, who did it in 13.3 seconds in Columbus, Ohio, in 1932. They, too, are listed in the Guinness Book.

Here are some of the other memorable records achieved by minor leaguers, even though they may have been obscured by their big-league brethren.

Perhaps the greatest legendary pitcher ever to throw a baseball and not succeed in the major leagues was Steve Dalkowski, a farmhand for the Baltimore Orioles. His strikeout ratio was awesome—1,396 in 995 innings in the minors in the 1950's and 1960's. Then again, so were his walks—1,345. Of the ten fastest men ever timed for the speed of their pitches, Dalkowski, at 93.5 miles per hour, was the only one who did not succeed in the majors. His minor league record was a mere 46-80.

Marathon Box Score

COMPLETION OF SUSPENDED GAME

ROCHESTER	ab	r	h	bi	PAWTUCKET	ab	r	h	bi
Eaton 2b	10	0	3	0	Grahm cf	14	0	1	0
Willms cf	13	0	0	0	Barret 2b	12	1	2	0
Ripken 3b	13	0	2	0	Walker lf	14	1	2	0
Corey dh	5	1	1	0	Laribe dh	11	0	0	1
Chism ph	1	0	0	0	Koza 1b	14	1	5	1
Rayford c	5	0	0	0	Boggs 3b	12	0	4	1
Logan 1b	12	0	4	0	Bowen rf	12	0	2	0
Valle 1b	1	0	0	0	Gedman c	3	0	1	0
Bourjos lf	4	0	2	1	Ongart ph	1	0	0	0
Hale ph	7	0	1	0	Lafrancs c	8	0	2	0
Smt lf	0	0	0	0	Valdez ss	13	0	2	0
Hazewd rf	4	0	0	0					
Hart ph	6	0	1	0					
Bonner ss	12	1	3	0					
Huppert c	11	0	1	1					
Putnm ph	1	0	0	0					
Grilli p	0	0	0	0					
Speck p	0	0	0	0					
Total	105	2	18	2	**Total**	114	3	21	3

Rch 000 000 100 000 000 000 001 000 000 000 000—2
Paw 000 000 001 000 000 000 001 000 000 000 001—3

E—Eaton, Logan, Bonner, Valdez. DP—Rochester 4, Pawtucket 3. LOB—Rochester 30, Pawtucket 23. 2B—Koza 2, Walker, Boggs, Huppert. SB—Eaton. S—Williams 2, Logan, Hart, Huppert 2. SF—Laribee.

	IP	H	R	ER	BB	SO
Rochester						
Jones	8⅔	7	1	1	2	5
Schneider	5⅓	2	0	0	0	8
Luebber	8	6	1	1	2	4
Umbarger	10	4	0	0	0	9
Grilli L, 0-3	0	1	1	1	1	0
Speck	0	1	0	0	0	0
Pawtucket						
Parks	6	3	1	1	4	3
Aponte	4	0	0	0	2	9
Sarmiento	4	0	0	0	2	5
Smithson	3⅔	2	0	0	3	5
Remmerswaal	4⅓	4	1	1	3	3
Finch	5	3	0	0	1	3
Hurst	5	2	0	0	3	7
Ojeda W,9-5	1	1	0	0	0	1

HBP—By Schneider (Laribee), By Parks (Eaton), By Aponte (Bonner), by Grilli (Barrett). WP—Jones, Hurst, Smithson. T—8:25.

N.Y. Times

Almost equally awesome in the minors was a Pittsburgh Pirate farmhand named Ron Necciai. On May 13, 1952, Necciai was pitching for the Bristol team, which represented the twin towns with the same names on the Virginia-Tennessee border. He struck out the side in the first inning and the first man up in the second in a game against Welch, West Virginia, in the Class D Appalachian League. The next man grounded out, but then Necciai, a 19-year-old righthander, began striking out everyone who faced him. After eight innings, he had a total of 23 strikeouts, one short of the maximum because of the one ground out. In the ninth, he fanned two more, thus matching the professional baseball record of 25. But there was more to come. The next batter struck out, too, but Necciai's catcher dropped the ball and the runner got to first. Under baseball scoring rules, the pitcher still got credit for the strikeout, bringing Necciai's total to 26. Necciai, for good measure, fanned the last batter, too, completing his no-hitter and 27 strikeouts.

(Left) The longest game on record occurred in 1981 in the minors—32 innings before it was suspended and rescheduled. Pawtucket won in the 33rd.

For Necciai, it was not just a one-night stand. His manager gave him seven days rest, then pitched him again. This time Necciai struckout 24. In his next games, he fanned 20 and 19. Those strikeouts and the ones he had pitching in parts of other games gave him a total of 109 in his first 42 2/3 innings. Necciai soon made his way up to the Pirates, but the experience was not a happy one. He won only one of seven games and was soon out of baseball.

For fielding, no one has ever made a more impressive play than the unassisted triple play by Walter Carlisle of Vernon of the Pacific Coast League, on July 19, 1911. Carlisle's triple play was different from the handful performed by other professionals in more than 100 years of baseball. The reason? He was an outfielder.

In the sixth inning that day in Los Angeles, Carlisle took off from shallow center after the ball was hit, dove desperately for the striking ball and caught it inches off the ground. Then after a couple of somersaults, he landed on his feet. The two men on base were in disbelief and had kept right on running the bases. Carlisle dashed to second and touched the base to get the lead runner, who had been heading around third, and then trotted to first to make the automatic out on the runner from that base who had passed second before Carlisle got there.

The best batting average for a full season of professional baseball was by Walter Malmquist, of York, in the Nebraska State League in 1913. After batting .241 in 1912, his average jumped to .477 in 1913—nearly 40 points higher than any major leaguer ever hit!

And finally, as spectacular as some major leaguers have performed in the big time, they even topped those records in the minors. Joe DiMaggio's major league mark of hitting in 56 consecutive games in 1941 is considered one of the—if not the—most impressive records in the books. As a 19-year-old playing for San Francisco of the Class AAA Pacific Coast League in 1933, DiMaggio gave a preview of things to come when he hit in 61 consecutive games. That, however, is not even the professional record. The mark is held by Joe Wilhout, of Seattle in the same league, who hit in 67 straight games in 1919. ■

Joe DiMaggio's famous swing is shown here in all its perfection as he hits a homer in Chicago against the White Sox in June, 1939. With one out in the 9th, he socked this pitch out of the park after having been laid up with a leg injury for more than a month.

JOAN JOYCE, SOFTBALL STRIKEOUT QUEEN, ONCE FANNED TED WILLIAMS AND HENRY AARON

With American women becoming more and more active in competitive sports, the question has emerged as to whether women will ever be able to compete successfully against men. That had never been Joan Joyce's goal, though as a softball pitcher her brief encounters with men have been quite remarkable. Perhaps no other pitcher, either male or female, in softball or baseball, can boast that he or she has struck out both Ted Williams and Henry Aaron. But Joyce did.

Now over 40 years old, Joan Joyce, who is recognized in the *Guinness Book* for pitching two perfect games and notching 76 strikeouts for the U.S. women's team in the 1974 softball world championships, and has been one of America's greatest athletes from the time she was in her mid-teens, never concentrated on proving her athletic talents against men.

"I can go out and play against men, and I have," Joan once told an interviewer. "But I don't see that as a big deal—or a goal."

In fact, when she recalled the day she pitched against Ted Williams, the Red Sox great batter, back in 1962, and collared him with her dazzling display of softball pitches that traveled as fast as 116 miles per hour, she was not out to embarrass one of baseball's greatest hitters.

"I felt badly about what I had done to Ted, who is a friend of mine," Joan said. "It happened right after he retired from baseball. He came to Waterbury (Conn.) and I was giving him stuff—dropping pitches after I set him up with rises out of the strike zone—that he had never seen in baseball. There were 10,000 people there, and I shouldn't have done it, even though he told me to pitch all-out."

The best Williams could do in 10 minutes against Joan's pitching was a couple of foul tips out of about 30 pitches.

Joan was 22 years old then and just beginning to completely dominate women's softball.

A blazing underhand fastball that rises or drops as it crosses home plate is Joan Joyce's pitch that fools the batters. In softball Joan has pitched over 130 no-hitters.

Sixteen years later, she faced Henry Aaron, the home run record holder with 755 in his career, under actual game conditions. Aaron had also retired from baseball, and was appearing for a softball team called Con's Kings. Joan threw six pitches to him during her stint on the mount. Aaron, very seriously, was trying to get a hit. He could not get his bat on any pitch.

Admittedly, Joan was in these games to help get women's softball some publicity. In almost a quarter-century as a softball player, however, she needed little publicity for herself. That came easy; few would disagree

that she was the greatest women's softball player ever.

As a pitcher in the amateur ranks for 22 years, Joan had a career record of 540-32, a winning percentage of more than 94 percent. Included in her victories were 130 no-hitters, 40 of them perfect games. At one point in 1975, her last season as an amateur, she had 229 scoreless innings on the mound, and she finished her amateur career with a 52-game winning streak.

Joan also had a career batting average of .325.

In 1976, women's softball gathered some of its finest stars and created the International Women's Professional Softball Association. It would be fair to say that the league was formed around Joan Joyce, the star and part-owner of the Connecticut Falcons.

Joan did not let the promoters down.

In the four seasons that the league was in existence, Joan had a 101-15 record as a pitcher, including eight no-hitters and three perfect games in her first two seasons. She batted an average of .290, and the Falcons won all four women's softball World Series.

Joan said that she could pitch softball for a long time, well past the age of 40. Though she has a relatively thin pitching arm, whipping it past her 5-foot-10-inch, 162-pound body, she had always been a durable as well as competitive athlete.

In 1980, Joan Joyce decided to concentrate solely on golf, and had some signs of success, earning more than $5,000 and finishing about three quarters of the way down the standings. But it may have been a tribute to her talents as a softball player that the pro league, without her, suspended its operations in 1980. That's how much she was missed. ■

THAT'S WHY THE LADY IS A CHAMP

Billiards Whiz, Loree Jon Ogonowsky

Concentration—that's what makes it work. Loree Jon shows the crowd what it takes to be a winner.

At age 15 Loree Jon Ogonowsky is the youngest professional pocket billiard player ever to win a championship.

The youngest is always a category that interests Guinness readers. The youngest champion in any category was 8-year-old Joy Foster of Jamaica who was singles and mixed doubles champion in 1958. The youngest swimmer was Gertrude Ederle who, at the age of 12 years 298 days, broke the womens 880-yard freestyle record.

Now along comes Loree, who became a world champion at age 15. She began playing pocket billiards, which most people call pool, when she was only 4 years old and could hardly reach the table. Playing in the basement of her home in New Jersey, she was ready to compete with all challengers. School was ignored and pool was favored. By the time she was 9, she realized she would have to get an education, so she retired.

While retired she would sneak downstairs when no one was around and practice. Then at age 11 she was persuaded by Bill Cayton of The Big Fights, Inc., to make a come-back and enter the 1977 World Championship where she finished 10th.

The following year she was 5th and 4th and 5th again and finally champion, beating men and women older than she is. Now she is headed for TV appearances and Bill Cayton has predicted that she will be a star because she is attractive and a great player. She only weighs 100 lbs. at 5 feet 6 inches and insists that success won't go to her head.

Girls at that age can take a cue from her. ∎

JAN TODD

World's Strongest Woman Advises Young Athletes: Avoid Steroids

Jan Todd playfully shows that she, like Kate Sandwina of earlier times can carry her 275-lb. husband around.

Jan Todd, who keeps setting new powerlifting records practically every time she competes, revealed in an interview with the Guinness Book editors that she is worried about athletes, especially women taking steroids to improve their performance.

"Steroids are very dangerous," Jan said, "for several reasons. They are male hormones and they make women more masculine, their bodies develop more muscle from the waist up, their voices may deepen, their menstrual cycles may be affected, and the changes may be irreversible. As for men, steroids will make them stronger, but not without certain potentially dangerous side effects.

"When some tests were made on pregnant rhesus monkeys by injection of steroids, female babies were born with partly abnormal sex organs and they were overly aggressive.

"Women will never have as strong arms and backs as men because they are built differently." Pointing out that women's muscles are much like men's in their lower bodies from the waist down, Jan noted that the records for women's squat lifts are not much different from men's because the legs and hips are used mostly, but that bench presses require upper body muscle, and there the differences are great.

"However," she said, "women can increase their strength and feel healthier by weight lifting and body building, and this helps, especially with young girls, in making them more self-confident."

Jan, though she was not required to do so by the current regulations governing powerlifting, submitted to a series of tests under the direction of an endocrinologist at the medical school at Emory University in Atlanta, where it was determined that she was not then and had not been using anabolic steroids.

The girls who are too thin and can't put on weight should look forward to a book that Jan Todd is writing, with recipes and exercises that tell you how to *gain* weight. She herself weighed only 165 lbs. when she began her weight-lifting career eight years ago, and reached 225 lbs.

at her peak. The records she set recently in Columbus, Georgia, were made at her greatest weight.

By training six days a week, Jan is able to reach world record level. Her latest bench press is 220 lbs., 545.5 lbs. for squat, 479.7 for dead lift, and a total of 1228.5 lbs. She was the first woman to lift, in the total, over 1000 lbs., then 1100 lbs., then 1200 lbs., and no one on the scene today can beat her. In a partial dead lift, as seen on a recent Guinness TV show, she has lifted 1230 lbs.

Jan recommends that girls try for college athletic scholarships which are more numerous now than ever before. The media and the athletic associations are now devoting more time and attention to women gymnasts and athletes of all types. Jan believes that working with weights can help improve a woman's performance in almost any sport.

"Russia is way ahead of us in weight training and establishing centers for studying the effects of strength training on men and women," Jan says. She is on the staff of the only such center in the United

Looking wistful with the bar she will have to lift, Jan Todd is thinking of setting another world record.

States—the National Strength Research Center at Auburn University in Alabama, where she works with her husband, Terry, who directs the center.

When she goes to meets in Europe, she meets weight lifters from behind the Iron Curtain, and has become good friends with the English-speaking super-heavyweight Russian champion, Vasili Alexeyev, probably still the world's strongest man, al-thought he has now retired from the competition.

How did she begin powerlifting?

It all began, a year before she was married, with an untossed caber, in a meadow by a Georgia millpond. (A caber is a long, slender log used for tossing at the Scotland Highland games.) The men were trying and failing to make the toss properly, her future husband reported, when Jan, then a young woman student in the philosophy department who had never seen a caber before, lifted it vertically, cradled one end in her hands, took a few steps forward, then tossed and flipped it so that the end in hands pointed straight away from

her in the exactly correct way. No giggling, no false modesty, just energy and skill.

"As near as I can tell, that was the day I began to love her," Terry Todd says about Jan Suffolk Todd.

Terry wasn't doing much in the way of sports at the time, other than a weekly workout in weights. But soon he had Jan practicing figure shaping with light barbells and dumbbells. Terry, a former national champion, had been a competitive weight lifter six years before, and now he began training again with Jan. At first, she used weight training as a way to stay fit rather than as a way to dramatically increase her strength.

However, once Jan learned about Katie Sandwina, the phenomenal German woman of the early 1900's who weighed 210 lbs. and juggled her 160-lb. husband in midair for a circus act, she began to take weight lifting seriously. Then in the "Guinness Book of World Records," she read about Mlle. Jane de Vesley who set a 392-lb lift record in 1926.

"I think I can beat that," she said,

and she did. But not before she and Terry had designed a program to build her overall strength. In the gym where she worked out, she expected trouble from the men she could outlift. But, to her surprise, she was accepted with warmth.

It was an uneven course. The first year, Jan hurt her back digging in the garden, had to stop training, had to go back to it slowly, then went stale, and finally got into top shape. More than a year after she began training, Jan broke the two-handed dead lift record for women at 394½ lbs. in 1975. (Her record in 1981 is 479.7 lbs.)

Neither she nor Terry like the "weak woman" image. Jan has always been a good runner and swimmer and player of games. Terry's younger sister, too, was more than a match in athletic contests with boys of her age. So, in the Todd household and family, strength for both sexes is desirable.

Jan Todd, the world's strongest woman, is steroid free and is as feminine and good-looking as any woman would want to be. ∎

LONGEST CAR COMPETITION

"No Frills" Version Home-Built by Reverend Sets 1981 Record

In 1927, when the Italian car manufacturer, named Ettore Bugatti made the "Royale" type 41, known as the "Golden Bugatti," 22 feet in length with a hood over 7 feet long, he probably thought he had set a record for all time in car length. In one sense he was right. This model, which continued to be built through 1931 (six were made and are still in existence), has stood up through the years as the *production car* of greatest length. All those "extended" cars built since then have been custom made.

A special Cadillac was constructed in 1975 for King Khalid of Saudi Arabia. Built in the U.S. by Wisco Corporation of Ferndale, Michigan,

it was 25 feet 2 inches long and cost several times as much as a standard Cadillac.

Then, in 1976, a New Yorker named Leo Weiser, president of the Automobile Club of America, Inc. had a special extended Cadillac measuring 26 feet 7 inches long built for him. It carried 43 gallons of gas, and was fitted inside with circular couches, a television, stereo, bar and refrigerator, telephone, video tape recorder, and 3 anti-theft systems.

To beat this record took some doing. Joel D. Nelson of Bakersfield, California, spent $100,000 "stretching" a 1976 Fleetwood Cadillac in 1979 to measure 29 feet 6 inches. It was fitted inside with *two* color-TV

sets, an 8-speaker stereo system, *four* phones, a safe, a video camera and recorder; and of course, a sink, refrigerator and bar. (Photos of this car appeared in the "Guinness Magazine" issue #1.)

Not to be outdone, the Reverend Gerald R. Manning of Middletown, Virginia "altered" his 1962 Chevrolet station wagon himself to a length of 32 feet 4 inches. He didn't bother to compete in luxuries for the inside.

Now, the race continues on. The Guinness editors have received phone calls about cars that are still longer. The rule, however, is that the car must obtain a license to be driven on the open road and that it actually runs (and can turn corners!) ∎

The Reverend Manning's home-built record-setter.

This special Cadillac belonged to the king of Saudi Arabia.

MOVIE STUNT MEN TEAM UP TO BREAK SOUND BARRIER AND LAND SPEED RECORD

A new land speed record of 739.999 miles per hour (or Mach 1.0106) was set by a rocket car on December 17, 1979 in a one-way stretch at Edwards Air Force Base, California. The driver was Stan Barrett, the owner was Hal Needham, and the designer was William Fredrick. On hand to witness the record event was Charles E. Yeager, Brig. Gen. U.S.A.F. Ret., who had been the first man to fly a plane faster than the speed of sound, in October, 1947.

Here is how General Yeager reported the event:

Gentlemen:

"The Guinness official photographer, Franklin Berger, was on hand to witness and photograph the first land vehicle to exceed the speed of sound at Edwards Air Force Base on Monday, December 17, 1979. Mr. Berger requested that I provide written testimony describing my judgment of the success of the endeavor.

"It is quite obvious that the Hal Needham Budweiser Rocket Car exceeded the speed of sound because of the rear wheels leaving the ground as the car achieved top speed.

"As the car approaches .9 to .94 Mach number, very strong shock waves will form on the nose, the tail and the wheel struts. When the car goes supersonic the shock waves which formed on the nose at lower speeds will move to the rear of the car. Evidently the choking effect of the shock waves under the car as they moved to the rear, lifted the rear of the car off the ground. I observed the track of the rear wheels on the supersonic run and the rear wheels were off the ground for 650-700 feet. A photo taken at the trap shows the rear wheels off the ground about 10 inches. Since the rear wheels weigh about 100 lbs. each and were rotating between

The Budweiser Rocket, powered by a 48,000-hp rocket engine and boosted with a 12,000-hp Sidewinder missile became the first land vehicle to exceed Mach 1, the speed of sound.

Franklin Berger

7-8000 RPM, they acted as gyros to keep the car from turning, directionally or laterally.

"Having been involved in supersonic research since the days of the XS-1 rocket plane, which I flew on the first supersonic flight on October 14, 1947, there is no doubt in my mind that the rocket car exceeded the speed of sound on its run on December 17, 1979."

In a previous attempt on September 9, 1979, the Budweiser Rocket had reached a speed of 638.637 mph on the Bonneville Salt Flats, Utah. But the salt surface was too rough to attempt to reach Mach 1, the speed of sound—about 750 mph depending on the temperature. The Air Force was therefore asked by Needham and Fredrick for permission to use the Air Force Flight Test center at Edwards.

"The salt flats were so rough," Stan Barrett stated, "the rocket tricycled, it lifted one rear wheel off the surface and bounced me around so much I could barely see." The runs at Edwards on Rogers Dry Lake were made on a 9-mile course. The car had a Sidewinder missile attached to provide an additional 12,000 horsepower. The only change made after the Bonneville run was to switch to a special hybrid rocket that doubles its horsepower. The hydrogen peroxide used at Bonneville produced 24,000 hp and the solid fuel substituted created 48,000 hp.

For the timing, three sets of devices were used in a system accurate to one hundred-thousandths of a second. Three sets of traps were set 52.8 feet apart with special sensors accurate to a millionth of a second. All timing was fed through a computer to ensure accuracy.

Designer Fredrick explained what happens as the car reaches supersonic speed. The vehicle must first pass through what is known as the transonic region from around 630 up to about 740 mph. "The drag coefficient triples in the transonic region, so it's almost like hitting a brick wall," he said. "It takes twice the power to go 750 mph as it does 600 mph."

The sound barrier is evasive. The speed of sound depends not only on altitude but on temperature. At Edwards the sound barrier was 741

BEFORE: The Budweiser Rocket is readied for its assault on the sound barrier. Rogers Dry Lake at Edwards AFB, California, was selected as the site when Utah's Bonneville Salt Flats, the traditional setting for land speed record attempts, proved too rough.

Photos by Franklin Berger

AFTER: Smiles abound after the successful supersonic run. Meeting the press are, left to right, driver Stan Barrett, owner Hal Needham, designer Bill Fredrick, and General "Chuck" Yeager. General Yeager became the first human to travel faster than the speed of sound when, on October 14, 1947, he piloted an XS-1 rocket plane to Mach 1.015 (670 mph) at an altitude of 42,000 feet.

mph at 32 degrees but 737.5 at 30 degrees.

While the 739.666 mph is a land speed record, it is not an *official* record, because a two-way run has to be made and the average speed of two runs computed, as wind can be a factor.

The men involved in the record run are experienced in racing, Stan Barrett, the driver and one of Hollywood's top stunt men, having served in the Air Force for four years.

Hal Needham, who owns the car, was the king of Hollywood stunt men and mentor of Barrett, and became a motion picture director later on. He wrote and directed the *Smokey and the Bandit* pictures starring Burt Reynolds. Barrett was Reynolds' stand-in. His career started as a wing-walker in *The Spirit of St. Louis*. Needham says "that was 25 years and 45 broken bones ago."

Bill Fredrick started with exotic propulsion systems as a teenager when he owned a 200-mph jet dragster. Now in the aerospace industry as a consultant on rocket power, he is a technical advisor to motion picture producers. ∎

ROLLER SKIING BECOMES LATEST SPORT

Pushing along the road with their ski poles, participants in the October, 1980 Roller Ski competition in Glens Falls, New York, had to use the same type of roller ski.

Cross-country skiing as a means of transportation, especially in military encounters, dates back over 4,000 years. Its enjoyment as a recreational pursuit began around 1860 in Scandinavia. Roller skiing, a snowless cross-country ski training pursuit, began in the same area of the world about a quarter century ago. Today, the once strange sight of a summertime cross-country skier striding up the road with barking dogs and laughing children in pursuit, and with motorists staring, is a picture seen with increasing frequency throughout the United States and Canada.

The first description of roller skis in the U.S. appeared in an August 9, 1967 newspaper article in the Rutland (Vermont) *Herald*. It described the then premier U.S. Olympic cross-country skiing ace, Mike Gallagher, and his colleagues preparing then for the 1968 Winter Olympics with summer training on Scandinavian roller skis. A quote from that article stated, "the roller skis are really amazing...they give almost exactly the same feeling you get on skis."

The earliest roller skis made were actually cross-country skis fitted with two wheels in the rear and a single wheel near the tip mounted in a cut-out portion of the ski. From these rather crude beginnings, roller skis have progressed to ultra-short platforms made of the latest ultra-light and strong space-age materials. Some are now even equipped with brakes.

Roller ski wheels are now much smaller but incorporate the same technological advancements seen in roller skates. A major difference from the roller skate's wheel, however, is the fact that the roller ski wheel will only roll forward. This allows you, especially with an assist from the ski poles, to easily propel yourself up hills. The front wheel locking rather than rolling backwards affords a stable platform from which to push yourself forward. The techniques of roller skiing, including single and double poling, are the same as for cross-country skiing. Roller skiing will sharpen your sense of timing and balance for full extension cross-country skiing.

The ski poles used with roller skis are regular cross-country ski poles with graphite tips recommended, as they stay sharp longer.

Just as cross-country skiing ranks at the very top of aerobic exercise pursuits, even ahead of running (because the upper body not just the legs are used), so, too, roller skiing ranks equal with its now equivalent as an aerobic activity. With people becoming aware of the many physical and emotional benefits of aerobic exercise, today roller skiing is growing not only as an off-season activity or when the snow is not available, but as a training device for cross-country skiers, and also as a recreational pursuit in its own right. Exercising the upper as well as the lower body, gentle on muscles, joints, and the spine, yet building strength and stamina, roller skiing is vastly superior to jogging for improving and maintaining total physical fitness.

The first roller ski races, naturally, were in Scandinavia. Today, they are very popular in Europe, a recent race in Karlstad, Sweden, having attracted 10,000 spectators. The first races in the U.S. were undoubtedly informal contests between Mike Gallagher and his Olympic teammates. Only very recently have organized roller ski races started to flourish in the U.S and Canada. The first "European" style roller ski race, in which every contestant used the same type of roller ski (thus eliminating equipment as a factor in the ultimate results), was organized by Tom Jacobs. Held in early October in Glens Falls, New York, when the Adirondack foliage is spectacular, the fourth annual Road-Ski Race recently attracted members of the U.S. and Canadian Ski Team, Quebec Ski Team, Dartmouth, Middlebury, and Johnson State Ski Team, plus many other ski clubs as well as recreational skiers. There were six classes including three for Junior boys and girls, Veterans, and Senior men and women. The Seniors raced 10 kilometers, while all others raced 5 kilometers. From a mass start, Art Kranick of the Adirondack Ski Club emerged the Senior men's winner in 33 minutes 20 seconds. Marilyn Buffing of the Grand Rapids, Michigan, Nordick Ski Team rolled to victory in the Senior women's division in 42 minutes 12 seconds.

The future of roller skiing is, indeed, very bright. As a total body aerobic conditioner, enjoyable recreational pursuit, cross-country ski trainer, and competitive event, its popularity in the U.S. and Canada is rapidly growing. It is also possible to foresee it develop as an alternative source of inexpensive self-propelled transportation. ■

STEVE McPEAK PLANS FOR MONTHS BEFORE VENTURING ON HIGH WIRE OR UNICYCLE

Photo by David Boehm

McPeak's most dangerous walk was ascending the cable car wire at the Zugspitze on the border of West Germany and Austria on June 25, 1981. He walked 3,117 feet up at a gradient of at least 30° to establish a record for the highest climb.

Steve McPeak is a daredevil. His ability to conceive stunts, engineer the required apparatus and establish records in feats of human endeavor has brought him recognition, both by his fellow stuntmen and by the editors of the "Guinness Book of World Records." McPeak, born in 1945, enjoys creating exciting stunts for television. In recent months several stuntmen have been badly injured as television cameras rolled, and many people have blamed the producers for putting them up to it. Since McPeak specializes in high risk stunts, Guinness asked its West Coast editor, Adele Millard, to interview Steve about his experiences. The story of how he became a stuntman and how he feels about TV stunts is both timely and interesting.

Adele: *How many records do you hold?*
Steve: I have three or four. I could accumulate more but my problem is David Boehm (American Editor of the "Guinness Book"). He doesn't let me accumulate a large number at one time.
Adele: *Do you mean he deliberately keeps you from doing this?*
Steve: Not exactly. He just won't accept some stunts for publication,

One of the greatest feats of all time is Steve McPeak's tightrope walk up the 1.7-inch cable from Rio de Janeiro, Brazil, to the top of Sugar Loaf Mountain—a total of 2,400 feet at a gradient of 25 degrees average. The climb was 675 feet in height, and it took 65 minutes.

so there is not much point in trying to establish records that won't get in the record book.

Adele: *Evidently some of the things you propose do have a very high risk involved. Guinness monitors all events carefully when it comes to potential danger.*

Steve: That's only been an issue since all the bad publicity about when the stunt shows began. It wasn't an issue last year.

Adele: *Yes, it was. I personally have been present at all the Guinness television programs since 1975 and I can remember the disputes between the producers of the shows and the book editor. Understandably, the producer wanted an exciting, entertaining program. That concept was fine with Mr. Boehm as long as there were reasonable precautions taken to avoid accidents and injuries. The current problems that television is having with hazardous stunts began more recently. Mr. Boehm has been concerned for many years.*

Steve: Well, I think that if the producers of the shows could do some of the things I do, they would think differently about it. You would never catch David Boehm getting up there on a high wire.

Adele: *I should think not! Why would he want to?*

Steve: Well, he's passing judgment on other people who can do these stunts.

Adele: *Steve, even a Wallenda can fall and get killed. It's not difficult to assess a stunt as to whether or not extraordinary high risk is involved.*

Steve: It never enters my mind, when I say I can do something, that anyone will disagree with me. I know there is a big difference between the amateur and the professional. I spend months thinking out each stunt. I can spend years experimenting through trial and error before building and rigging an act.

There are many factors that I have to consider in planning an event. I try to think of all the negative elements first. Then one by one I cope with them and get everything down on paper. I spend a lot of time doing that, and even more time in engineering and building the apparatus for the act. Some of the problems take

years to work out. I have faith in the strength of my hands and in my ability to create a spectacular act that is safe. Some stunts I would never attempt. I'd never take a chance with them.

Adele: *You mean that there are stunts other people have done that you think are too dangerous? Even for you?*

Steve: Yes, because the one thing I never count on is luck. There is no way I would ever hop a motorcycle and jump over a ramp. I have to know without a doubt that at all times I am in control of what I am doing. I'm not about to take any flying leaps on big high jumps and just hope I can make it.

Adele: *The records you have set all appear to be dangerous, at least to me. For example, how were you so sure that you could control the walk over Yosemite Falls?*

Steve: I spent months looking over Yosemite. I saw the jagged rocks, and the way the water rushed into the falls. It was a terrifying experience just considering it. Then the time came when I started to think about a

43

For this walk across the Yosemite Valley in California, first Steve had to get the wire 300 feet across and tightened up—a major engineering achievement. The height above the valley floor was 2,625 feet, almost twice as high as the Empire State Building.

always a lot of turmoil and there were not many places around for me to get peace and quiet. I liked anything that involved physical activity so I started climbing trees. That became my quiet place. It was a world of my own...a little fantasy world. And the climbing taught me how to overcome my fear of heights.

Adele: *Did you really have a fear of heights when you were a child?*

Steve: I sure did! I remember the first time I climbed up a tall tree. I was scared to death. I grabbed at the first limb and wouldn't look down. The same with the second, the third and so on. I just had to get to the top of that tree. I couldn't look down but I couldn't back down from doing it, either.

Adele: *Why? If you really were that frightened, why did you go on?*

Steve: Well, I guess it was because I wanted to get to the top.

Adele: *Sounds familiar. This is the motivation mountain climbers give.*

Steve: It's a lot like mountain climbing, really. It's a great sensation to set a goal, feel fear at the idea of doing it and then overcome that fear. The first time I got to the top of the tree, sat there and then looked down, I just couldn't believe the feeling that made me want to climb. I climbed everything I could—trees, barns, silos. Anything, just to get away from the damned world.

Adele: *Did you ever think of going into a room and closing the door?*

Steve: There would be nothing to look at. Sitting on top of the tallest tree lets me see everything in all directions. I was about eight years old when I started climbing. I remember I worked my way up a barn from the edge of its shingles, a 60-degree incline. It was rough but I got to that top.

Adele: *Didn't your father see you perched on tree tops and walking on the roof of the barn?*

Steve: No. Not very many people look up. During an ordinary day most people look only at the things that concern them. Unless there is a reason for it, why would anyone look up? Anyway, in that barn I created a whole new world for myself.

Adele: *How did you do that?*

Steve: I had rigged an apple box onto the track in the barn that was used to lift bales of hay up to the loft. I put a length of baling wire on the box and around the wheel lift and got into the apple box. I could then pull on the

way of doing it. I knew I could handle it and worked it out in my mind. Then and only then did I feel I had control enough to make the walk.

Adele: *Was the walk over Yosemite Falls harder than the cable walk in Brazil from Rio to Sugar Loaf Mountain?*

Steve: Yes! The walk in Rio was tough. However, after Yosemite Falls, my mind could handle just about anything. I was nervous and anxious while I was considering it, but I wasn't really scared in Rio because I had been successful with the Yosemite walk.

Adele: *You feel then that all you have accomplished has been the result of a natural progression? Each time you have done something a little different it's also been a little harder?*

Steve: That's the only way it should be done if you are going to attempt a stunt that involves risk. When I was young I was all guts because I had never experienced pain. As I got older I saw enough of the world to know pain and disaster exist. Then I started being practical and began to think in terms of safety. Everyone should apply common sense to each thing he does. If you are going to climb a 100-foot ladder, you don't start on the fifth rung and then skip to the eighth. You start at the bottom and go up one rung at a time.

Adele: *Let's go back, Steve, to the time you first discovered your fascination with heights. Was it during the period you worked with your father as a lumberjack in the state of Washington?*

Steve: That was only 15 years ago. It started long before, when I was a child. I'm the oldest of seven children. In my big family there was wire and make a circuit of the loft. Well, one day I was going for my usual ride when the boards that supported the track broke. The apple box stopped 15 feet from the end. The wood had shattered and there wasn't anything supporting the track. I knew I had to get off without the whole thing collapsing. One thing I knew for sure was that I better not holler for help! So I used my feet and the wire and got back to the other side.

Adele: *That must have been a horrifying experience for an eight-year-old child. I bet you kept your feet on the ground for awhile after that.*

Steve: Nope, you'd lose your bet. The next day I went back and built a scaffolding. There were a lot of nails all over the barn and plenty of pieces of scrap wood. I hauled this scaffolding up to the broken edge and fixed the track. That was my first engineering job. I just put it all together and knew I did it right. Even then I had faith in my ability because I wasn't afraid to use the apple crate any time I felt like it.

Adele: *How did your father discover what you were up to?*

Steve: During that time I would go for walks around the edge of the silo. The silo was 30 feet high and there was a two-inch ledge all around the top. I was carrying my cat, "Groucho." I named him that because he had a little black moustache just like the actor. There we were, old "Groucho" and me, trotting around the silo when my dad looked up and saw us.

Adele: *I can imagine his reaction. Did you get punished?*

Steve: He didn't do anything to me, but you can believe I never heard the end of that story. He found out about everything then, apple crate and all.

Adele: *Since your dad was a lumber-jack all your climbing must have made him aware that you were going to be a chip off the old block.*

Steve: Oh, sure. I worked my way through college with my jobs in the logging camps. It turned out that I was a pretty good rigger, probably my greatest asset. I learned how big operations worked, so it's easy for me to rig and operate the apparatus I need for my stunts. That includes all the high-wire acts, and stilts as well as unicycles.

Adele: *I would think a circus would be a natural place for you to find a steady employment. Instead, you perfer to work occasional special events and television shows, most of which are riskier than work in a circus. Why?*

Steve: I used to work in a circus years ago. I found out that for me it was a dead-end street. There wasn't nearly enough money and a lot of work. No recognition; you fall and kill yourself, they bring in another high-wire walker. The steadiness of the job can really become a hazard. I did an act two times a day, three times on Friday, Saturday and Sunday. It was routine. It's easy to become careless then. Now each stunt I do is being done for the first time. Even if it isn't, I have trained myself to look at it that way. It keeps me alert, so I know that each time I have to prepare myself mentally and physically.

Adele: *How do you prepare? Perhaps some future record-holder reading this can learn from what you do. Is it something special, Steve?*

Steve: Special? No, I don't think so. I relax physically and key myself up mentally. I think of everything that could go wrong. Then I think of the right way to handle each possibility. Then I go out to do the stunt. I know I am going to do it. And I do! ∎

Photographs by Franklin Berger

Steve McPeak smiles as he climbs up a wire at an angle of about 37° at Santa Cruz Amusement Park.

(Left) Steve McPeak seems to be walking on thin air, but actually he has strung and stanchioned wires into the snow-covered peak of the Zugspitze and an equally high peak opposite and is walking 181 steps at a height of 3,150 feet above the ground.

JIM KING RADIO ANNOUNCER TURNS FUND-RAISER BY PERFORMING STUNTS FOR RECORDS

by Jim King

As a radio announcer my career spanned 15 years and ended in April, 1980, just before I set the roller coaster record of 368 hours. The last four years were spent as program director and after-noon disc jockey at WDLP radio in Panama City, Florida. Wherever I worked—at radio stations all over the country—I loved getting involved with the public. At first the productions I put on seemed different and exciting, but as time went on, they didn't seem so exciting any more. That's when I started looking for more of a challenge. No one on staff wanted to be directly involved in bizarre stunts, and since

At the top of a long drop, Jim King is in the midst of setting a new roller coasting record of 368 hours for 3,475 miles without stopping, breaking his old record by 200 hours. Three of the 15 days and nights were spent sleepless during torrential rains and lightning storms.

radio stations seldom have money for outside help, that left me to do the stunts if I wanted to attract listeners and raise funds.

The first stunt I came up with was a promotion for the local fire rescue squad. I had myself confined to a pit 4 feet wide, 7 feet long and 6 feet deep. I shared it for a week with a number of large python snakes. I took my microphone into the pit with me and broadcast during the whole week. I guess I must have had a good following because we got donations of over $10,000. This was in 1972, before I grew my beard.

I had one close call. A python wrapped himself around me and wouldn't let go. I didn't know exactly what to do but I just lay on the floor totally relaxed while the snake uncoiled. Even while this was happening the other snakes were crawling around me and they never stopped. I had pretty exciting week.

Because I got such a tremendous response to this stunt, the local rescue squad asked me to do a stunt the following year. This time I decided to get buried in 16,000 pounds of ice. We built an ice house with 300 blocks of ice, leaving just enough room for me to lie down and get up on my knees. The ice house, which was 7 feet long, 46 inches wide and 46 inches high, was then wrapped in insulation and covered with tarpaulin to preserve the ice and to prevent it from melting on me. Direct sunlight was kept off the ice house by a tent. I was completely sealed inside along with my radio equipment, a telephone and food enough for seven days. I kept broadcasting even when the temperature, which was 32° in the daytime, dropped to 24°-26° at night.

Although I didn't need the rescue squad, they were stationed beside the ice house 24 hours day in case for an emergency. The low temperature inside kept me from sleeping. Of course, I was wrapped in heavy clothing, but this was a rough deal. After the week was up I came out, I experienced numbness in my ankles and feet for four months. I had rasied a great deal of money for the local rescue squad with my broadcasts but I wouldn't like to do that again.

It was in 1978 that I first got into the "Guinness Book of World Records" for roller coaster riding at Miracle Strip Amusement Park at Panama City Beach. The stunt was also to raise money for Muscular Dystrophy with the Jaycees.

A record for roller coaster riding at that time was held by three men from Virginia who had gone for 100 hours in June, 1977, and had covered 1411.2 miles. The record had been going up by leaps and bounds. The Guinness Book of 1965 came out with the first record for roller coasting at 24½ hours. By 1968 the record had gone up slightly to 31 hours set by four men in Wales. This held until 1974 when three men and a

Jim King was not always alone as he rode the Miracle Strip Roller Coaster for a record in Panama City, Florida, in 1980.

woman rode on the Kings Island roller coaster in Cincinnati, Ohio, the highest, fastest roller coaster in the world, for 36 hours covering 546 miles in 728 circuits. This roller coaster, which is called "The Beast," has a 141-foot-high drop and a speed of 64.77 miles per hour now, but it may not have been so fast in 1974. Compare this with the Panama City model I rode which has a drop of 80 feet and a speed of 60 miles per hour.

When I got in touch with the Guinness office in New York, I was told that records were being broken all the time in the interim between editions, and that the 1979 edition was going to press August 15, 1978. My ride started August 28 and ended September 4 so I couldn't make it into the 1979 book, but I did become the first man ever to ride a roller coaster for a full week—168 hours exactly. The distance I covered was 1946½ miles. During the ride I hallucinated off and on due to lack of sleep and extreme heat, but I had no other serious problems.

I didn't want my record broken, so once again I got in touch with the Guinness office in New York, and I was told that someone was going after my 168-hour record so I was determined that I would set a record that nobody would ever break, and I would do it in time to get into the 1981 Guinness Book.

I rode the Miracle Strip again to raise money for the same people. The Jaycees had a doctor on hand again to check my physical well-being during the ride. I started on June 22, 1980.

For 15 days 8 hours (368 hours) I stayed on that roller coaster despite everything. The toughest times during the ride were three days and nights with torrential rains during electrical storms. Later I was told that a tornado had touched down during these storms about 3 miles from the Miracle Strip. During the storms I found it impossible to relax or sleep. With all the water accumulating on the tracks, the braking system didn't work and the operator was unable to stop the coaster when it struck bottom. The cars just hydroplaned across the brakes and flew through the terminal area at full speed and up the hill again. I never had a chance to relax. The storms really wore me out. As I look back, I think it was sheer determination and will power that got me through.

The ride, which totalled 3,475 miles, consisted of 6950 laps and ended on July 7, 1980, just in time to make the "newly verified records" section in the back of the 1981 Guinness Book. The ride was of great personal satisfaction to me and earned the Panama City Jaycees a national number one rating.

I have given up my radio career now and I'm spending my full time helping people. In January, 1980, I attended Gulf Coast Community College and received training as an Emergency Medical Technician. After graduating in May, I started work at Bay Memorial Medical Center Ambulance service as a registered EMT, and am now attending paramedic school, specializing in advanced cardiac life support. In emergency medicine I plan to use my skills as a radio announcer to help promote emergency medicine in this community or wherever I go. ■

CAN BLOWING BUBBLES MAKE YOU A BETTER KISSER?

**Ask The Champ,
Susan Montgomery Williams**

Susan Montgomery Williams blows a bubble that would foil any bully if popped in his face.

When the judges at a bubble gum blowing contest in Florida asked Susan Montgomery Williams to stop blowing her bubble because their "gumputer" wasn't big enough to measure it, she knew she had clinched the prize with her 19½-inch giant. But this bubble was only one of many that have won her bikes, a stereo, clothes, money and a place in the "Guinness Book of World Records."

Imagine the wheel of a bicycle and you will understand Susan's amazing talent, because that's about how big she can blow them and that's why she's the champ.

As a student, Susan always participated in school sports, games, and contests, both in and out of school. She holds other titles as well as bubble-blowing champ. In 1973 she was the Hula Hoop champion of Fresno, California, and she became the Fresno Boxing Queen in 1979.

Susan travels all over the U.S. entering contests and teaching her technique. Once she was given a free scuba diving lesson for showing the divers how to blow bubbles underwater. "You do it the same way you do out of water, except you use more pressure because when you're underwater the pressure makes the bubble start stretching up so you go floating back up."

And on another occasion she was asked by a fireman to give his wife lessons to improve her kissing because "...she can't kiss worth a darn."

Can bubble blowing get you out of a tight spot? It helped Susan. She was able to discourage a bully by blowing a bubble in his face. Gaining a momentary advantage when her assialant looked behind him, she was able to blow a big enough bubble in time to have him turn back right into it, popping it all over his face and covering his eyes, nose and hair. Freeing herself from his grip and taking advantage of his momentary blindness, she was able to blow a popping sound, thus fooling him into thinking it was gunfire and frightening him off. "I call it my .38 caliber bubble," Susan remarked.

Now, Susan is spending most of her time caring for her new baby girl, Bonnie Marie Williams. Even in the delivery room, Susan blew bubbles through the entire labor and delivery.

How do you go about improving your own bubble blowing?

"I noticed that most kids who would try to blow a bubble would put a whole pack in their mouth and try to blow a bubble with the sugar in it and throw it away when the sugar was gone. But I have found out that you can blow a bigger bubble when all the sugar is out." Susan suggests washing the gum in warm water instead of chewing the sugar out. The sugar crystals keep the gum from fully expanding. She thinks it's also better for your teeth and health if you're going to be practicing a lot.

When you start blowing bubbles bigger than your head, Susan recommends pinching the bubble and stretching it away from your hair. Covering your face with a layer of moisturizer or lotion will keep the bubbles from sticking to your face.

Now that you have the inside information, why don't you try it? ■

A beautiful double bubble—concentration and patience are needed to achieve this degree of skill.

Susan poses with a classic triple bubble. Lip practice helps improve her kissing technique.

255,389 DOMINOES TOPPLE FOR HEMOPHILIA FUND IN EXCITING SPECTACULAR PATTERNS IN JAPAN

In domino-toppling events, dominoes have been made to dial long-distance telephone calls, they have cooked eggs, walked under water and traversed waterfalls, traveled up 12-foot ramps and down again, played music. Dominoes have been set in patterns so complex and beautiful that they could not have been imagined a few short years ago.

The record set in 1980, under the auspices of the National Hemophilia Foundation, took place in Japan, when two young men from the suburbs of Chicago managed to topple a total of 255,389 dominoes in 52 minutes in a mind-boggling spectacular. They spent five weeks in Hakone, in the shadow of Mt. Fuji, setting up the dominoes to shoot rockets up, climb rainbow patterns and run on straightaways without stop while branches raced off into intricate formations to perform feats while the mainstream carried on. John Wickham is an engineering student and Erez Klein is a mathematician, both still in university— and they're not satisfied yet. They want to try for a million in 1981.

It all began in ancient China—not domino toppling, but the game of dominoes. It was introduced, to Europe in the 1800's. Dominoes got their name from their resemblance to the black-and-white cloaks worn by Cathedral Canons.

The Innuit Eskimos are fierce in their play with dominoes, gambling wildly, and have been known to stake and lose their wives in play.

Erez Klein and John Wickham stand in the midst of more than 250,000 dominoes in Hakone, Japan, just prior to their record-breaking topple in August 1980, which took 5 weeks to set up and 53 minutes to fall.

In politics and warfare, the "domino theory" has been widely used to describe situations in which the downfall or collapse of a single entity triggers a succession of similar casualties. The sport of domino toppling has transformed it into a positive theme and image, making it a spell-binding event to watch on television. Beginning 8 years ago a young mathematics student from the University of Pennsylvania, Bob Speca, first appeared on the scene and for TV showed he could tumble large quantities of dominoes with a single push for the edification of excited audiences.

His first record of consequence was 11,111. Speca went on to 15,000 (which can be seen on tape at the Guinness Museums, as can the 255,389 topple), then 22,221, and step-by-step to a 100,000 try in New York City on June 9, 1978. He would have made it, had it not been for a newspaperman who leaned over the balcony causing some cards to fall out of his pocket and knock down about 2,500 dominoes in a row below, before the domino train could reach them. So Speca had to be satisfied with a record 97,500.

A year later Wickham and Klein in Illinois toppled 135,215, but didn't get into the Guinness Book because in the interim between editions Michael Cairney of London, who had been in dominoes since 1977, came to Poughkeepsie, New York, and under the auspices of the National Hemophilia Foundation, had toppled 169,713, with displays that Speca had never experimented with. Using all colored dominoes, cameras and rockets, Cairney made history and started a new wave of domino tumblers.

Both the Guinness editors and the Hemophilia people had ruled that only real dominoes may be used, and a level surface is absolutely necessary. The Foundation's slogan is "Topple Hemophilia" by toppling dominoes—and its fund has grown tremendously since it began its sponsorship of the sport in 1977.

Finding a way of clotting blood not only cures those who have a hereditary blood disorder, but will aid in treating many other diseases. The clotting factor can be removed from whole human blood, concentrated into a powder and then can be

Dominoes set off a model of an Apollo rocket in the 1979 World Domino Spectacular sponsored by the National Hemophilia Foundation.

Michael Cairney, 1979 Guinness Book record-holder, takes a congratulatory call dialed by domino power after his tumble of 167,713 dominoes in Poughkeepsie, New York broke all previous records for toppling dominoes.

reconstituted at any time almost anywhere. This helps in treatment of burns, all sorts of accidents, with hemorrhages, anemia, tetanus, hepa-titus, leukemia and many infections, to just name a few uses.

So, "hemophilia toppling" will be of major benefit to mankind. ∎

51

ICE-CREAM-EATING CHAMPION VOWS
"NEVER AGAIN"

by Geri Martin

Vanilla is the flavor most favored in general and "least sickening" for contestants in ice-cream eating contests, according to Robert J. Howard, owner of the Dean Dairy in Waltham, Massachusetts, where the world record was set in 1977.

Bennett D'Angelo, the 270-lb. record-holder, who swallowed 3 lbs. 6 oz. of unmelted 12° ice cream in 90 seconds, and is proud of his world record, vows nonetheless never to do it again. Bennett feels that no one is going to break his record, and even he can't match it again. No one in the five intervening years has been able to surpass Bennett, although many have tried.

When a person swallows an enormous quantity of ice cream or swallows it quickly, usually a headache, a beating of the nerves in the temples and forehead, is likely to ensue. But Bennett did not get a head throb in 1977, although he felt pretty sick at the end. His face was numb for half a day, and he discovered that the cold had loosened a tooth—and the filling had fallen out.

Despite Mr. Howard's insistence that vanilla is most popular, Bennett feels that he would have liked it better and perhaps done better with chocolate ice cream.

Actually, Bennett could not have set the record if he had not been consuming the hand-packed variety of ice cream. Machine-packed ice cream is only about half as heavy. Mr. Howard says that a half gallon of his homemade hand-packed is equal in compressed weight to a whole gallon or perhaps 5 pints of the average machine-packed.

At Dean Dairy, the champ is memorialized in both the sign above and with the "Big Benny" sundae named after him.

After Bennett set the ice-cream-eating record at the Dean Dairy he got immortalized when a gigantic banana split was named "Big Benny" after him by Mr. Howard.

Bennett, who now weighs 289 lbs., and eats a pint of ice cream normally every night after dinner, works as a machinist in nearby Watertown. When he made the "Guinness Book" he received invitations to compete in other contests, one of which included a free trip to San Francisco.

The 1977 event was staged by Dean Dairy with a great deal of hoop-la for the six weeks previous. Two local television stations and the popular Boston disc jockey, Mike Adams, covered the whole 12 minutes, with Adams giving a blow-by-blow description. There were 28 contestants, including three women, but no children registered. All the contestants were sick afterwards.

The Dean Dairy is not new—it began in 1725 as The Dairy Farm in a house that is still standing across the way from the present quarters. In 1917, the name was changed to Dean Dairy, but no ice cream was sold until 1919. When Mr. Howard bought the place in 1964, he went into ice cream in a big way, selling both soft (Dairy Whip, he calls it) and regular, as few shops do. Ice cream has to contain 10% butter in order to legally use the name. Dean's now sells 29 flavors, but vanilla is twice as popular as the next most wanted flavor, chocolate. May is the most popular month, and a weekend in May will bring 5,000 customers to the big spotlessly clean Dairy on a Sunday alone.

Mr. Howard had started holding eating contests just for fun. Since 1977 he has been contacted by ice cream sellers in 37 states asking for information on holding contests, how to promote them successfully, how to ask for and obtain signed waivers, how much the contest may cost, how many gallons get consumed, and what publicity might result. Tourists, having read about Dean's in the "Guinness Book" often stop in for their cones and sundaes, Mr. Howard stated.

His everyday customers include large contingents from colleges in the Waltham area—namely Bently and Brandeis.

Will he run any more contests? "Maybe we'll build the largest sundae," Mr. Howard predicted. ∎

Robert Howard, owner of Dean Dairy, and his friends eat as they watch Bennett prepare for a record attempt.

Warming up, Bennett D'Angelo starts with a cone or two then quickly escalates to an all out attack on a banana split.

All photos by Geri Martin

THE ISLAND WITHOUT PICKPOCKETS

by Burton H. Hobson

No one worries about pickpockets on Yap! In case you have never heard of Yap, it is a 38.7-square-mile island in the western Pacific Ocean. Today, it is part of the U.S. Trust Territory of the Pacific Islands.

Yap's claim to fame, as recorded in the *Guinness Book of World Records,* is its use of stones as currency, the most massive coins ever known. These incredible stone disks vary in size from "small change" of less than 9 inches in diameter to massive "cartwheels" 12 feet across. Even a medium-sized stone coin is worth one wife or an 18-foot canoe. Produced centuries ago, the limestone from which the discs were made was quarried on the Palau Islands about 300 miles away. Transporting the raw stones in small boats involved great danger and stormy passage or lost lives. This increased the value of the individual pieces.

Once the stones reached Yap, they had to be worked, without being broken, into their round shapes and a hole drilled through the center so that the coins could be carried on poles. With only crude implements to work with, the carvers took as long as two years to shape a stone.

The remaining stone money can still be seen propped against trees and walls along a muddy road on the edge of the village of Colonia. The coins are not moved around any longer, but ownership is transferred from family to family when land is sold or other goods traded. Everyone on Yap knows who owns each piece and the history of the coin.

Stones are not the only unusual items to have been used as currency in various parts of the world. ∎

Pamala Hollie/NYT Pictures

These holed stone discs, used for money in the Yap Islands of the Western Pacific can be traded for one wife or an 18-foot canoe, depending on size.

Cowrie shells were used as currency the world over during ancient times.

For 900 years or more, tea cast into bricks was used as currency in China, Tibet and other Asian countries. These bricks were stamped with the value and the name of the issuing bank.

Stone money from the island of Yap. Note the hole in the middle for carrying on a pole.

The Swedish 1644 10 daler plate money piece is the world's largest metal coin, weighing 44 lbs., measuring 14 inches by 24 inches by ½ inch. Its purchasing power was equal to two cows.

Copper, cast in the form of a cross, is still used to purchase brides among the peoples of isolated northern Rhodesia.

Originally produced by North American Indians as ornaments, shell discs on a string were later accepted by European colonists and the Indians themselves as money.

BEES' BUZZ WORSE THAN THEIR BITE, SAYS COOKE, WHO SET BEE BEARD RECORD

Don Cooke of Terrace Park, Ohio wears a beard sometimes—a beard of bees. It's 17½ inches long, reaches from his ears down to his waist, and consists of 21,000 live, buzzing Italian-type bees, a Guinness world record.

Who ever dreamed up the idea and why does Don Cooke perform this feat? Guinness sent a reporter to interview him.

Guinness: *How long have you been growing bee beards?*

Cooke: I'm 69 years old and I've been working with bees for 60 years. But I didn't get started with beards until 1969 when I was 58.

G: *How did it happen?*

Cooke: My dad was a farmer and florist who kept 20 hives of bees. I've grown up with the bees and feel comfortable with them buzzing around me. So when a friend who runs the Ohio Honey Festival asked me to wear a beard as an attraction (the man who did this the year before couldn't be found again), I volunteered.

G: *And you continued doing it?*

Cooke: Yes, I've done this more than 80 times at the Ohio Honey Festival and 123 times in all. The Ohio Festival each year attracts more than 150,000 people.

G: *Were you scared the first time?*

Cooke: Not scared, but maybe apprehensive. I did it to show the general public that they have nothing to fear from bees. Bees are not out to sting you, and they are not monsters. When properly handled, bees and people can get along friendly-like.

G: *When you grow your bee beard are the bees treated with something?*

Cooke: No. The bees come from a regular hive—nothing special. But

Don Cooke enjoys having a warm beard of buzzing bees, as long as they don't get in his eyes, ears and nose.

they are well fed in advance, so they're not hungry when released.

G: *Do you put something on your face?*

Cooke: Nothing at all. What attracts the bees and keeps them on me is the queen bee which is tied to my chin in a little gauze cage. She gives off an odor—pheromone is what it's called—which is attractive to the worker bees. I do put cotton in my ears and nostrils to prevent bees entering.

G: *Do they tickle?*

Cooke: They tickle if they wander up around my eyes—I don't like them so close. In any case, I am able to block out most of the feeling and relax my skin.

G: *Don't you ever get stung?*

Cooke: Sometimes I get stung, but I don't show any signs of pain, so those outside the big cage I'm enclosed in don't even know. However, if I lose control I ask my helper to come in and remove the stinger from beneath my skin. He does this by blowing smoke on the area of the sting to cover the "alarm odor" which the bee releases with the sting. The smoke also is designed to destroy the bees' communication and in that way avoid further stings.

G: *Can you put on this show at any time of the year?*

Cooke: Yes, but weather has a lot to do with the temperament of the bees. They become more aggressive with a change in atmospheric pressure. For example, they don't like lightning in the air.

G: *How do the bees know you want them to form a beard?*

Cooke: They don't. Curiously, when we let them out of the hives, they don't react in the same manner each time. Sometimes they don't want to climb up far enough toward my sideburns to form a full beard, so I end up with more of a "bee collar" unless my helper guides them with the aid of 3x5 index cards.

G: *Do you have trouble getting the bees to go back into the hive?*

Cooke: Not usually. My helper uses the index cards to "shave" them off in little batches at a time. Of course, they follow the queen bee, so the first thing we have to do is unstrap the queen from my chin and put her back where she belongs in the hive. Then if they don't want to go—and like me better than their queen—we have to vacuum them off. The vacuum confuses them, but doesn't seem to hurt them.

A big luscious kiss from his wife while his bee beard clings on, is the highlight of Don Cooke's demonstration. Mrs. Cooke is said to be allergic to bee stings. Brave woman!

Assistants to Don Cooke seem impervious to all the bees swarming around. The beard is made by pushing the bees off the hive with a card so they join the queen bee attached to Don's chin.

G: *Your business is bee-keeping for honey, isn't it?*

Cooke: Yes, my wife processes and markets all the honey for us. She collects the honey between midnight and 4 A.M. She is also a honey judge at fairs. She's allergic to bee venom and doesn't work in the hives, but she does take some risks sometimes—she comes and gives me a kiss while I'm wearing the bee beard!

G: *Does your wife go to all your beard sessions.*

Cooke: Not all of them, but she does sometimes talk over the public address system and tell the crowd what is taking place in the cage where the thousands of bees are flying around and about me. My 8-year-old granddaughter got into the act once when she came into the cage and kissed me.

G: *Has being in the Guinness Book changed your life?*

Cooke: Yes, I get a lot of attention, and I think the TV shows helped get me more publicity. But the big thrill came in another way. When I was a boy, we kids used to have an expression "see you in the funny papers!" Well, thanks to Guinness I got into the Sunday "funnies" when the color comic strip used an illustration of me. ■

GUINNESS ON TELEVISION :
THE UNEXPECTED IS WHAT YOU GET WHEN CONTESTANTS BET ON RESULTS

When you watch a game show on television you are likely to get the impression that it's unplanned and easy to get onto videotape. True, it's unrehearsed because when betting on results is at stake and money is paid out, the networks insist that no one know the right answers in advance. On the Guinness Game Show, which ran on NBC and affiliated stations for 48 weeks (including repeats) in 1979-80, the contestants had to state if they thought the contenders for records would succeed or would fail in their attempts. This gave the producers problems that other shows never have. Adele Millard, who was there as Guinness representative watching all the shows, was asked to tell what unexpected events occurred at the tapings which took place in the studios of KTLA in Los Angeles over a period of four weeks.

Because the producers could not rehearse the contenders before they went on the air the following is a prime-time example of how everything can go wrong on TV.

The people chosen to attempt to establish records had submitted breath-taking accounts previously. Their claims were backed up with the required credentials. The walk-throughs showed promise, but as soon as the cameras were in position, and started shooting, events that could go wrong, did. Possibly the technical problems could have been compensated for, but what is to be done when the star act—a man who could chin over a bar 10 times in 2

Javier Gomez, from Colombia, broke the record of jumping rope 80 times on a high wire 33 feet above the ground while the cameras were off him, and then could only do 54 when the TV crew came back. *(all photos, courtesy of General Foods Corp. and Ogilvie & Mather, Inc.)*

John Brown, physical education instructor from Cal State, Fullerton, attempted to shovel a mountain of coal weighing 1,120 pounds into a hopper in 42 seconds to break an existing world record. He fell far short, but created great clouds of dust.

minutes using only two fingers is in front of the camera and can do only one chin-up, and this turned out to be the best of the day's acts? We did the only thing we could. We acknowledged that the day's shooting was a waste, put it in the can, and filed it.

On the next show, Javier Gomez, selected for his agility, was checking out the equipment he was using to break the record of jumping rope 50 times on a high wire 33 feet above ground. Producer Michael Hill and Guinness Editor David Boehm asked him how many he thought he could do.

"100" was the reply.

"Don't do more than 80 then," said Hill.

So Gomez jumped 80 times without a miss. When the time came for the actual performance, Javier did set a record...54 jumps! The 80 jumps could not be used on the air because it was done during the un-official session of testing the wire without the camera.

Toby Hoffman had the surprise of his life when he discovered he made Guinness history just by being helpful. Toby, of Santa Monica (whose photo is on the cover) had the job called "safety precaution" for the show. He stood by at each event, tested equipment, stayed near the daredevil contenders with emergency rigs and was as helpful as a 6-foot, 230-lb. muscleman could be. Toby happened to be standing by the doors of the set when the bricks for the lateral brick lift were brought in. Toby listened to Boehm explain the rules for this event to the contender. Illustrating the directions, Toby lined up the bricks, placed his open palms on each end and pressing inwards laterally lifted the 16 bricks, weighing 96 pounds. After the bricks were set down, the smiling Guinness editor congratulated an astonished Toby for setting a new record! Turning to the contender, Boehm explained that this was the way the lift was to be done and that he had to better Toby's

record on the air. The contender could not duplicate the feat!

One of the records attempted was to shovel a mountain of coal weighing 1,120 pounds into a hopper in less than 42 seconds. The coal miner from West Virginia who tried was only able to do 500 lbs. despite his muscles and frantic shoveling. Coal dust rose in clouds as he worked and slowly settled on everything on the set. The cameras picked up the action despite the black cloud of dust. At the end of the alloted time it was apparent that the only record set was that Editor Boehm, stop-watch in hand, turned 5 shades darker in 42 seconds!

Don Galloway, the host for the show, was surprisingly adept when he demonstrated an upcoming event. But even the imperturbable Don's cool was shaken when he threw a Frisbee and the electronic device which was used to measure the speed registered 150 m.p.h.! It may not have equaled the skills of Superman but it came close. The timing device was checked and found to be malfunctioning. After a quick repair, the Great Galloway changed back into the mild-mannered charming host while Charlie Duvahl, the Frisbee contender, went on to throw it at a more realistic 60 m.p.h. And his partner, Steve McClean, caught it in his bare hands, thus setting a world record.

A Cherokee Indian attempted a feat of skill in marksmanship by trying to throw 12 tomahawks into 5 playing card targets mounted on long ends. He failed to hit more than one target and make it stick while the camera was on him for the Guinness Game Show, but there is an excellent chance he can do it at another time. After his part in the taping was over, the crew went out to a parking lot to set up for an outdoor event. While members of the staff were watching the outdoor episode on the monitor in the Green Room, gradually they became aware of a rhythmic thump-thump sound in the background. Upon investigation the noise was found to come from the Indian still throwing tomahawks and hitting the target almost every time! For an hour the filming continued despite the mournful thump of the tomahawk hitting the playing cards. Finally all was silent. It was time to go home and the shredded playing cards, mute testimony to the persistence of the Indian contender, were picked up and thrown away.

Walking barefoot at any time can be hazardous. Boehm was unhappy about the walking-on-glass event, not only because of possible injury to the claimant, but also because some young viewer might be tempted to emulate the contender. Host Don Galloway described the stunt and then issued strong warnings to the TV audience about the folly of trying to duplicate this act. Paramedics and an ambulance stood by while the broken bottles were set down in a 10-yard-long stretch. Then with the cameras on him, the contender moved so lightly and quickly that he traversed the glass-strewn path in 20 seconds setting a record without a cut on either of his feet!

Komar, who already held several Guinness records including walking

The happy smiles turned to gloom when judge David Boehm announced that no record was set by Joy Lieberthal, 9-year-old math wiz. Her father Ed Lieberthal, lecturer and author, stood by. West Coast editor of Guinness, Adele Millard, assisted Mr. Boehm.

on coals at a temperature of 1,494° F. (and whose story appears in issue #1 of the Guinness Magazine) was not so lucky when he attempted to break his own record. In the parking lot a 25-foot runway of oak chips was started burning early in the day so it would reach 1,500° when it came time to do the fire walk. Komar uses mental discipline, akin to self-hypnosis, for this amazing act. This time though, with the audience restless, he could not maintain the necessary mental control, and was distracted. His trance broken, he could feel the scorching pain on the bottoms of his feet, and so he hurriedly left the burning path. The producers had thought this record would be in the

bag because Komar had never before disappointed the TV cameras.

The Guinness Game Shows have proved that bringing a new dimension to a television program opened up a Pandora's box of unexpected results. This made the Show so exciting since no one, not even the producers and editors, knew what to expect. Television exposure did more than just provide a show-case for a person's attempt to gain recognition, it brought the Human Achievements chapter of the Guinness Book to life. A wide range of contenders...cheese makers, car salesmen, students, teachers...tried to show that anyone can establish a record as the best in the world in something. ■

CROCODILE SWALLOWS OUTBOARD MOTOR

The estuarine crocodile pictured here is not the largest nor the heaviest nor does it have the largest skull, but it got into the "Guinness Book" because it swallowed an outboard motor and killed itself in the process.

Do you know the difference between a crocodile and an alligator? Both are members of the *Crocodilia* class of reptiles, and are equally at home on land or in fresh or brackish water. Both are cold-blooded, air-breathing, spiny animals covered with protective "scales" which are like bony plates. Both lack a good mechanism for regulating their body heat, so their temperature rises and falls according to the surrounding air or water. Both have paired limbs that make for awkward crawling. Both have long tails, and in fact they look so much alike, you can't really tell them apart unless you look into their snouts and examine their teeth.

The alligator (sometimes called the American alligator) has a slightly longer tail, a broader, shorter snout and its lower jaw teeth fit into pits in the upper jaw instead of into marginal notches, as in the crocodile.

The estuarine crocodile, which lives in salt or brackish water, is the largest species of reptile in the world, measuring 14 to 16 feet in length and weighing 900 to 1,150 lbs. As they get older, they tend to get half as heavy again.

Tests carried out in France to determine the jaw strength of a 120 lb. crocodile revealed that this saurian could exert a crushing pressure of 1,540 lbs. On this basis, a crocodile weighing 1 ton could exert a force of nearly 13 tons. Human jaws can exert a pressure of 500 lbs.

The "official" record for length, which was registered in Sri Lanka (formerly Ceylon) where many such crocodiles are found, is 19 feet 7⅛ inches, and this fellow was accurately measured because he was a notorious man-eater, and was shot and killed.

This record, in fact, is eclipsed by an Australian crocodile. The greatest authentic measurement recorded for an estuarine crocodile is 28 feet 4 inches for a bull shot by Mrs. Kris Pawlowski in Australia, in July 1957. Under normal circumstances this measurement would be rejected because nothing of this monstrous saurian was preserved, although a photographic record existed until 1968. However, as Mrs. Pawlowski's husband, Ron, is one of the world's leading authorities on this species, and farmed the estuarine crocodile at Daruma, Mount Isa, Queensland to 1969, this record must be regarded as one with a high probability of accuracy.

Mr. Pawlowski said that the only means of dragging such a bulky weight on to dry land away from tidal reach would have been by tractor but, as one of these vehicles wasn't conveniently at hand, this was completely out of the question! He also added that the freshly severed head was so heavy that he could not move it.

The most famous saurian in this category was an alleged 33-footer killed in the Bay of Bengal, India, in 1840 which had a girth around the belly of 13 feet 8 inches—the body was obviously distended by internal gases—and weighed an estimated 3 tons. Fortunately, the skull of this giant reptile was preserved and later presented to the British Museum (Natural History), London. This croc must have measured just over 25 feet 6 inches in life.

Earlier, in 1823, another huge estuarine crocodile measuring 27 feet was killed by Paul de la Gironiere (1854) and George R. Russell at Jala Jala, near Lake Taal, on the island of Luzon in the Philippines, after a struggle lasting more than six hours. The crocodile, a notorious man-eater, had apparently attacked and killed one of the Frenchman's shepherds while he was crossing a river, and Paul de la Gironiere had decided to avenge his death. In the monstrous saurian's stomach were found a horse, bitten into seven or eight pieces, plus about 150 lbs. of pebbles, varying from the size of a fist to that of a walnut, and the head weighed 450 lbs. before the ligaments were detached. ■

UNDER A BLANKET OF ASH

AN EYEWITNESS ACCOUNT OF THE EFFECTS OF THE MT. ST. HELENS BLOWOFF

by Diana Kerman
Guinness Correspondent in the Pacific Northwest

It wasn't the biggest volcanic eruption in history (that was in 1815 according to the "Guinness Book of World Records") but it was big enough to qualify as the largest in the United States in recorded history. Mt. St. Helens, located in the Cascade Range in the state of Washington, about 50 miles northeast of the city of Portland, Oregon, was called Tah-one-lat-clah, meaning Fire Mountain, by the Klickitat Indians of the area.

The volcano had lain dormant for 123 years when it began in 1980 to show signs of becoming active and violent. March 1980 brought Mt. St. Helens awake with seismic activity and explosions of steam and ash. By the beginning of May a bulge of nearly 1½ square miles, 330 feet high, was building and expanding at the rate of about 5 feet per day. The big blast which broke out of the north side of the mountain came early Sunday morning, May 18, 1980, with a blast 500 times greater than the 20-kiloton atomic bomb that fell on Hiroshima.

Ash and steam brought darkness to Yakima, Washington, 85 miles to the east causing havoc with breathing and tying up car, rail and air traffic. However, Portland, Oregon, the City of Roses, the largest city near the explosive force, received only a light dusting of ash on that May 18. During March, when news was received about the activity on Mt. St. Helens, there had been an air of excitement and expectation at the thought of an active volcano at one's doorstep. Some Portlanders enjoyed

Mother Nature gives and takes away. Over 100,000 acres of tall fir trees were defoliated and toppled by the gaseous eruption of Mt. St. Helens.

AP Laserphoto

viewing the early steam plumes from the windows of their city's high-rise buildings. They found it exciting and beautiful to watch the steam plume move slowly across the sky. The city of Portland didn't realize what the Fire Mountain had in store.

May 18 was a beautiful, sunny day in Portland. Some Portlanders heard or felt the big 8:32 A.M. eruption. Others were first alerted by listening to the news. Numbers of Portlanders rushed to their hilltop parks or skyscrapers to view the unusual sight of an exploding volcano. However, subsequent eruptions and heavy ash fallout brought unexpected changes to the lives of all Portlanders.

When the ash fallout was heavy, it looked as if the city was being blanketed with a dusting of gray snow. But, this snow did not melt—it just became heavier as it was mixed with rain. The ash fell everywhere—on each car, roof, leaf and rose bush. Citizens were told to wear masks, and those with respiratory problems were cautioned to remain indoors. Cars stalled as ash was blown into their mechanical filters where it clogged the motors, and Portlanders were told to change their air filters frequently. Even the outdoor bank machines became inoperable as ash jammed their moving parts.

The ash seemed to stick to each place that it touched. Great water pressure and a stiff broom were needed to sweep the heavy ash into piles to be left at the curbs. The ash was not to be washed into the sewers as it was already jamming the storm drains, which needed to be emptied by shovel and the silt deposited as land fill. Fortunately ash was found to be a good fertilizer and could be left on the trees and shrubs. Gutters on the roofs of the houses, however, were filled with a heavy deposit of ash which mixed with rain and this most effectively stopped up the downspouts of each home. Home owners had a job cleaning out gutters to prevent clogging. Even a year after the major eruptions, ash could still be found on the lower leaves and vegetation. The rain has washed the ash from the roofs back into the gutters, which needed to be cleaned again. As Portlanders discovered, unlike snow, ash does not melt!

Portland, each June, hosts a Rose Festival. 1980 was no exception in spite of the Mt. St. Helens' explosion.

Where to begin? The clean-up job after the volcano exploded was made more difficult when the ash mixed with rain after a shower. The dust became a thick sludge that clogged sewers and chimneys. Motorists were stopped in their tracks when ash-clogged air filters stalled engines.

Waste from the volcano had filled in some of the Columbia River with debris—mostly logs—and some of this had washed into · the feeder rivers, including the tributary that flows through the very middle of Portland. Since a special event in the Rose Festival is viewing ships of the visiting Canadian Navy and U.S. Coast Guard and playing host to the sailors, there were doubts about the event and the navigability of the rivers. These were overcome and the smaller ships were able to sail in from the Pacific Ocean, although the sailors had to be placed on a three-hour alert, in case Mt. St. Helens blew its top again and landlocked the ships. The sailors and Portlanders enjoyed the festivities of the Rose Parade and the Fun Center, even if Helen loomed in the background.

As with any catastrophe, there is an opportunity for enterprising citizens to make a few bucks. A proliferation of souvenirs—T-shirts, authentic ash in bottles, and bumper stickers warning "Mt. St. Helens—watch your ash" quickly caught the eye of the tourist in Portland. The *Harmonic Tremors* became a new singing group. Residents of the state of Washington aptly erased the W from their license plates so the world would know they lived in the land of "Ashington." Even Hollywood got into the act. The movie *St. Helens*, starring Art Carney, is the story of rebellious Harry Truman (no relation) who refused to leave his home on the mountain.

New vocabulary sprouted up among the non-geologists who live in the Pacific Northwest. The man on the street talks freely now about "mudflow"—meaning debris (mostly vegetation) mixed with water which flowed into all the streams—and "pyroclastic flow"—meaning volcanic material such as ash which has been exploded from a volcanic vent.

Damage from Mt. St. Helens included human life, loss of crops, timber and property valued in the range of $2 billion. Recently, the Army Corps of Engineers announced that it will cost $939 million and take 15 years to clean up the devastation brought on by the eruption of Mt. St. Helens.

Geologists are unable to predict exactly the future movements of the mountain, which is rising once again and may reach its previous peak, or may explode again. But one thing is certain—the future of the mountain is unpredictable and Portlanders are now ready for anything that may come down the mountain or out of the sky. ∎

TALLEST WATERFALLS IS ALSO THE QUIETEST

by David F. Hoy

When the Guinness TV crew wanted to film Angel Falls in Venezuela, the tallest waterfalls in the world, I was offered the opportunity of going along in my capacity as Managing Director of Guinness. I jumped at the chance, although I had little idea of what was in store for us. Just prior to this, I had accompanied the group to some tapings at Leeds Castle in Kent, England, where we had measured the world's tallest dog and witnessed the high leap by a German shepherd RAF dog, and heard the voices of the world record loud shouters.

At Angel Falls, I expected, we would hear the tremendous roar of water falling 3,212 feet. In that I was disappointed, for although tons of water fell every second, it is a comparatively fine spray that reaches the bottom. That means there is not the thunderous noise of cascading water normally associated with large waterfalls. In fact there is an eerie silence in the vicinity.

Angel Falls is located in an area that is extremely inhospitable and inaccessible between the Orinoco and Amazon Rivers in northeast Venezuela. Water cascades in a torrent with a continuously changing pattern in the 14 seconds it takes to fall from its peak to the canyon that is its base, and as the stream turns to spray, it is criss-crossed by rainbows. The Indian name for the Falls means "water coming out of the sky" and it is a most apt description, for frequently the top is invisible in the clouds. As I gazed at this multi-hued spectacle, I

Despite the large overhang at the top and outcrop growths of thick jungle vegetation, Angel Falls was ascended by a group of four in 1971.

David F. Hoy

Ruth Robertson

An airplane can hardly be seen as it flies in front of Angel Falls, 3,212 feet high—15 times higher than Niagara Falls.

When our little group came in by helicopter from our encampment 18 miles away, I wondered if we could land near the Falls. The cloud cover limited visibility, and I remember that when Jimmy Angel had gone back two years later to the Falls area looking for gold, his landing had been successful but the plane had bogged down in the marsh and had to be abandoned. It had taken Jimmy and his wife and companions 14 days literally to hack their way through the jungle to their base camp 14 miles away.

We had to fight treacherous wind currents with our three helicopters, to find a place to land that was not too near the Falls or the fast-flowing river that leads to the Falls. A small patch had been hacked out of the jungle with machetes near the base of the Falls, for use as a base camp. Our skillful pilots managed to maneuver their choppers inches over the tree tops and land in the clearing—a dangerous 25-minute flight from our resort camp at Canaima.

Once established there at the base, our helicopter, a Bell 212 and two Hughes 500 C's, flew continual sorties throughout the day until they had filmed the Falls in more detail than anyone ever had before. It had not been readily apparent from photographs that there is a large overhang at the top, which makes climbing up to the top next to impossible. Despite this and despite the fact that much of the rock facing is concave, interspersed with outcrop growths of jungle vegetation, the Falls face was climbed in 1971 by a team of four. It took them nine days to make the ascent.

A brave group of climbers had volunteered to try this from the top down for our cameras. They managed to get part way down, nearly 1,800 feet, but the mists set in and we didn't want to leave them on the wall overnight. Miraculously, operating under extremely difficult conditions, our pilots managed to get them off safely.

To be at the bottom one minute and then five minutes later be standing 3,212 feet higher (15 times higher than Niagara Falls) on top of Angel Falls, in the clouds, made me realize how excited Jimmy Angel must have been when he came upon this incredible superlative of nature. ■

felt I was sharing the awe and majesty that entranced the first man to discover the Falls, Jimmy Angel, the American aviator who was passing by 46 years before, in 1935.

It is difficult to find a way to the Falls by air, let alone by foot. The jungle itself is very high, dense and extremely wet. Officially the rainy season lasts only from May to November, but the high humidity ensures that it is wet most of the year.

Moreover, the jungle is home to all kinds of pesty creatures—especially insects—huge flies and mosquitoes, as well as ants which crawl up your legs if you stand too long in one spot. If the ants sting a human, they cause a 24-hour fever. These insects and man are in a constant battle with deadly tarantula giant spiders. The Indians thought that the area which they call Auyán-Tepuí (Devil Mountain) is inhabited by legendary beasts, and, to ward off the evil spirits, they paint their faces red.

A BIG RED ROCK NAMED "BABY"

by Gail Peterzell

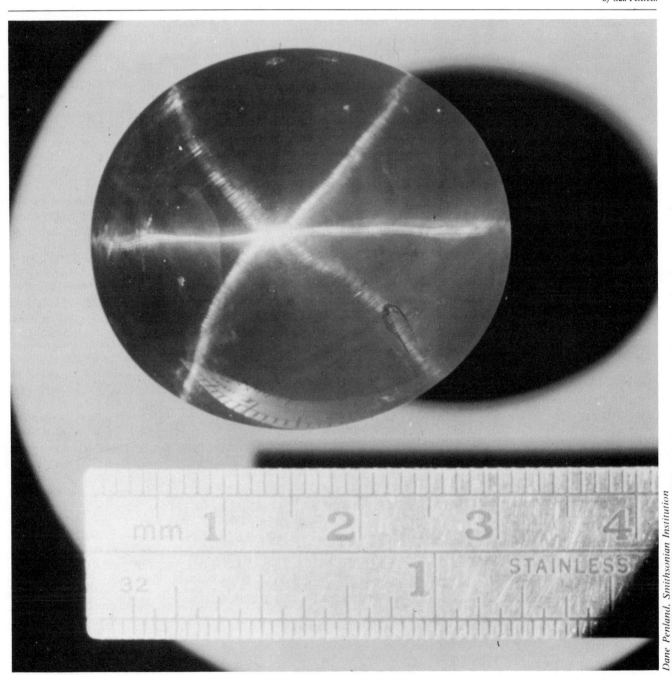

Rosser Reeves' "Baby" with magnificent star at home in the Smithsonian Institution.

J ewels! Romance, intrigue, big bucks, murder, beauty—and a myriad of other explanatory words for one of the biggest businesses in the world.

Rosser Reeves, the legendary chairman of the board of a giant advertising agency, found, bought, loved and donated "Baby," the biggest star ruby in the world to the Smithsonian Institution.

In a brief, mystifying interview with Rosser the following emerged—this reporter learned as much about the Rosser Reeves Ruby as any jewel owner will tell. The Rosser Reeves Ruby is now exhibited happily in Washington, D.C. In the summer of 1957, Mr. and Mrs. Reeves were on their way back to New York from Australia. Comfortably ensconced in the Hotel Phoenicia in Beirut, not even dreaming what was to happen, they had a call from Abdul. Abdul was a jeweler friend of Reeves' in Istanbul, who had sold gems to Rosser before. Now they learned he had called Rosser's New York office with an urgent request for a return call. So, when they met in Beirut Abdul told them of a big upcoming auction in Istanbul, Turkey, that he guaranteed would be full of surprises and serious buyers would be coming to Istanbul. Rosser was intrigued and learned that the world's largest star ruby, 138.72 carats in weight, had surfaced.

There had been a legend for 300 years that such a star ruby existed somewhere in the world—but where? Now Rosser knew Istanbul was the place and he and his wife went there immediately. The auction was already in progress, and the ruby was being bid on. Rosser, knowing the one and only reason he had come, asked if he could take a minute to see the ruby. With two official guards and the ruby in hand, Rosser went out into the sunlight to inspect this treasure. He had two seconds to set a price—which he did. Amazing but true, Rosser Reeves won the gem with a bid that was less than the top price he would have paid. (This price has never been divulged.)

The auctioneers never tell who owned a stone, when, why, or for how much unless the owner cares to tell. King Farouk and his sister had some jewels in the auction and Rosser feels certain Farouk owned the ruby—but who knows?

Since the stone had disappeared several centuries ago it is difficult to track the journey of the ruby. Now, the ruby was to be the capstone in the Reeves collection. Rosser sent a messenger for U.S. dollars to be transferred to Swiss francs in a numbered account in Switzerland. It took 3 or 4 days to conclude paying for it—we will never know how much it was, but today it is worth 1½ to 2 million dollars.

The Reeves happily tucked "Baby," their new gem, into a small case, and Rosser came home with the case in his pocket. Years went by, years full of fun and problems with "Baby."

One time Rosser was lunching at the famous New York restaurant, "21," before leaving for London. On the plane he opened "Baby's" case, and the gorgeous jewel was missing. When he arrived in London he immediately called Peter Kreindler, the owner of "21," and was told "Baby" had been left on the bar. Peter told Rosser to relax—they had found it and put it away. Vastly relieved, Rosser then continued his assignment in London. When he returned to New York, Peter handed "Baby" back in a lipstick-stained, scotch-taped facial tissue.

Rosser kept the stone through thick and thin. Then in 1965 Murph the Surf burglarized the American Museum of Natural History in New York City and stole the entire jewel collection. Murph was soon caught and the Museum got back all the jewels except the fabulous 100-carat DeLong star ruby. Finally John MacArthur, insurance billionaire, ransomed the DeLong stone for $25,000, and returned it as a gift to the Museum.

While Rosser was busy reading the *New York Times* story about the DeLong star ruby, he came across a quote by the jewel curator of the Smithsonian Institution, Dr. George Switzer. The quote simply stated that the DeLong was the world's largest and also finest star ruby. Rosser immediately wrote the renowned Dr. Switzer:

"If you are in fact the jewel curator of the Smithsonian Institution please do not go around making irresponsible statements such as the one I read in the *New York Times*. The DeLong ruby is *not* the largest and finest star ruby in the world—I own the world's largest and finest. Sincerely, Rosser Reeves."

Two days later Rosser's secretary came into his office and said that Dr. George Switzer was on the telephone. Dr. Switzer somewhat abruptly asked about the Rosser Reeves Ruby. Rosser told him about "Baby," and his answer was "Oh, my God, it's surfaced."

"Where is it now?" asked Switzer.

Rosser said "I'm rolling it around on my desk blotter."

"When can I see it?" asked Switzer.

"Any time," answered Rosser. "Come to New York."

Rosser set up an appointment to meet the next day for lunch at "21".

Dr. Switzer was an hour late, but was so eager to see the gem he didn't bother to shake Rosser's hand. Although Dr. Switzer never drank, at this moment he had a stiff drink, he was so dazzled by the gem. The sunlight from the window made the ruby shine like the superstar it is.

Dr. Switzer asked Rosser if he knew the world's big rubies by name. Rosser answered that he did, and proceeded to name the big three. The enthused Dr. Switzer immediately countered with "No—there are four, you forgot the Rosser Reeves Ruby. Please donate it to the Smithsonian right away—we must have it."

Actually, "Baby" had become a bit of a burden to the Reeves family. Rosser had lost the gem four times, hidden it in books, and he felt, just in general, "Baby" was slowly driving the family crazy. It was clear that "Baby" needed a new secure home, so in 1964 he donated the Rosser Reeves Ruby to the Smithsonian with certain clauses in the deed of gift. The ruby had to remain at the Smithsonian and would be known forever as the Rosser Reeves Ruby.

The secret is now revealed—the real name of that big red rock is "Baby." ∎

MAGIC MOVIE MOMENTS

Stunt men tend to risk their lives and limbs, but usually rehearse until they know exactly how to avoid injury. Yet once in a while, the unusual occurs.

This occurred in 1941 during the shooting of *They Died with Their Boots on:* Bill Mead was one of those stunt men hired as horsemen to ride in a cavalry charge. As it happened, Mead's horse tripped as he rode alongside the star of the picture, Errol Flynn. Mead had the presence of mind to fling his drawn sword forward to avoid falling with it, but by incredible mischance the hilt of the sword stuck in the ground and Mead fell on the tip of the blade, impaling himself. Mead had not practiced sword flinging.

* * *

Talking of stuntmen, Kevin Desmond in his "Guinness Book of Motorboating Facts and Feats" tells the stories of spectacular stunts with motor boats.

In the 1920's, Malcolm Pope during a race in Lake Wales, Florida, jumped over a dock, sending the boat 10 feet skyward and 50 feet forward. The crash proved too much for the bottom of the boat which split.

Then, in the 1960's a five motor-boat stunt fleet called the Johnson "Super Stingers," each powered by Seahorse 20's, put on their most spectacular stunt. They got their motorboat to go up and over a ramp, and through a wall of fire made of straw and lattice work, which was burning a mixture of gasoline and kerosene.

The movie *Live and Let Die,* the eighth James Bond film, needed a boat jump. Jerry Comeaux, 29, driving a Glastron GT-150, powered

Mary Pickford and Douglas Fairbanks canoeing in the Pickfair swimming pool on their honeymoon.

Culver Pictures, Inc.

Jerry Comeaux driving a Glaston GT-150, making his record jump of 110 feet at a take off speed of 56 mph on location for the James Bond movie "Live and Let Die."

by a 135-hp Evinrude Starflite on an isolated waterway in Louisiana in October 1972, made a then-record jump of !10 feet at a takeoff speed of 56 mph.

The current record is 138 ft made in 1978 by a Johnson-powered Cobra for the Burt Reynolds picture *Gator*.

* * *

Movies came to California instead of to Florida because a man named Al Christie won the toss of a coin. Christie was the chief director of a company making Westerns in New Jersey in 1911, and was tired of having to simulate sagebrush. The owner of the company thought Florida would be better but agreed to abide by a heads-or-tails decision. Christie won and took the company to California.

He found a derelict roadhouse on Sunset Boulevard in L.A. which looked suitable and cost only $40 a month to rent. This building was converted into a studio in October 1911. Today it is the site of the West Coast headquarters of CBS.

The name "Hollywood" had been applied to this area as early as 1903, and it had nothing to do with the holly bushes that had been imported from England. It was the name of a ranch belonging to Mrs. Harvey Henderson Wilcox, wife of a real-estate developer. She simply liked the name Hollywood when she heard it. It was the name of the summer house near Chicago of a woman she had

The longest jump achieved by a powerboat has been 120 feet by Peter Horak in a Glaston Carlson CVX 20 Jet Deluxe with a 460 Ford V8 engine (takeoff speed 55 mph) for a documentary TV film "The Man Who Fell from the Sky," at Salton Sea, California, on April 26, 1980.

met on the train going east in 1886, and she adopted it for her ranch. Then 17 years later the village of Hollywood that surrounded the ranch became a municipality.

Beverly Hills became the suburb of Hollywood in 1919 when Douglas Fairbanks rented the home of sporting-goods manufacturer Syl Spalding, a 36-room house on Summit Drive. At that time Beverly Hills was mainly agricultural land given over to the cultivation of beans. Only one house stood between Fairbanks'

rented property and the sea seven miles away.

Early in 1920, he bought a hunting lodge adjacent to the Spalding mansion and rebuilt it in a style befitting his new bride, Mary Pickford.

Called "Pickfair" after the first syllables of their names, it remains a magnet for movie fan tourists as Beverly Hills' most regal establishment. Lived in by Mary Pickford, it was put up for sale in 1980 following her death. The 45-room mansion sold for the asking price of $10

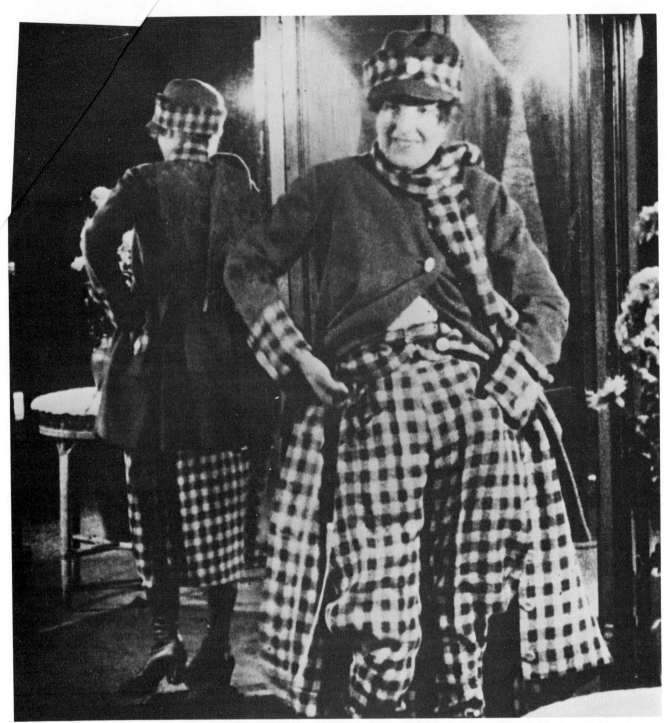

Do you know who this is? Would you call her the most beautiful woman in the world? Here at age 16 in a Swedish advertising short called "How Not to Wear Clothes," is the woman who conquered Hollywood, Greta Garbo.

million—a bargain for property in the area.

* * *

Greta Garbo set hat styles in her films though she was the star who made least effort to be a style-setter. The enormous fur collars she wore in the 1920's were intended to conceal her long neck. Garbo's berets, which she only wore off-screen, became a universal fashion in the 30's and they made a comeback in 1967 after Faye Dunaway had worn one as the 30's woman gangster in *Bonnie and Clyde*. Garbo was also instrumental in introducing the diagonally placed Eugenie hat dipping over one eye, worn by her in *Romance* in 1930. ∎

DON'T BITE THEM, SELL THEM

"Anyone Want To Purchase My 27½-Inch-Long Thumbnail?" Asks Young Indian Photographer

Shridhar! Stop biting your nails! Being a dutiful son, that's just what he did. That was 29 years ago and he hasn't bitten them since. But he hasn't cut them either.

Do you have any idea how long human nails can grow in 29 years? Well, from 1952, when Shirdhar Chillal of Poona, India, was 15 years old, until 1981 his nails have reached an aggregate length of 180 ½ inches. That is about 26 inches, more or less, for each finger on his left hand with his thumbnail taking the lead at 27½ inches.

Just what can you be besides a Guinness recordholder with 108½ inches of nails on your left hand? Not much. Let's hope his mom didn't have her heart set on his being a brain surgeon or a Swiss watchmaker. We all know how the world feels about one-armed paperhangers, so that's out, too. According to Shridhar, though, you can be a press photographer for the Indian Government. As you can see in the accompanying photos, Shirdhar, with a mitten (custom-made) covering his hand and protecting his nails, is able to hold his camera and shoot. But what about loading and focusing?

Does he sleep with his hand under the covers or out? How does he put his hand through his shirt sleeve? We at Guinness asked him these biting questions and Shirdhar replied that with his left hand encased in the mitten, he can keep his nailed hand anywhere, and with a zippered sleeve, he has no problems. Shirdhar claims that daily routines like shaving, bathing, etc., are a snap and he does them without any assistance.

Why would you voluntarily plague your life with this impediment? There

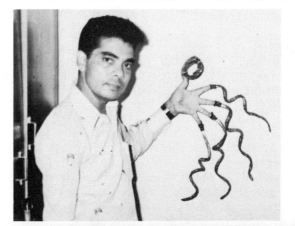

Vincent Price playing "The Fly?" No—Shridhar showing us how he holds his camera and umbrella.

is a small corps of single-minded men with determination and the desire to set themselves apart from the herd. Just what did happen that day 29 years ago when Shirdhar Chillal of Poona, India, stopped biting the nails on his left hand? Maybe nothing. We'll never know, but we do know that Shirdhar is now con-

sidering selling his nails. As a matter of fact, he has been considering this for quite some time. He's just putting out feelers now, and finding supplementary employment in fairs and bazaars that pass his way, while he's waiting for the person with just the right urge to have long fingernails, even if they're not his own. ∎

"WELL DONE," McDONALD'S SAYS TO COOKS WHO GET BACHELOR'S DEGREES IN RARE COURSE

by Susan Saiter Anderson

Some may call it cow college, or even go so far as to label it a "Moo U."; but students at this midwestern university take their classes seriously. Many of these students already have a bachelor's degree, but they're in classes all day for two weeks and poring over their books at night because they are working towards their "bachelor of hamburgerology" degree.

This is Hamburger University, located in Elk Grove Village, Illinois, where each year more than 2,000 selected people, mostly managers or franchise-holders of McDonald's restaurants, take courses ranging in length from one day to two weeks. Though there's little clowning around here, a bronze statue of Ronald McDonald stands in the hallway, as a reminder to students that McDonald's restaurants' success formula is serious enough business that they can get college credit here. Though this isn't really a college in the full traditional sense, many Hamburger U. graduates can transfer their credits to a four-year college.

Hard work does not remain unrewarded; at the end of the two week advanced operations course, one lucky student is awarded a golden chef's hat for contributing the most to class discussions. Another student walks away with a ceramic abstract model of a hamburger, for highest academic honors.

Thinking big, and small, has been the secret behind the success of the McDonald's empire. It stretches clear around the world, holding the Guinness World Record for largest restaurant chain, with more than 6,000. From California, home of the original McDonald's to the midwest, where the first franchise restaurant still operates, to Canada, Europe, Japan and Hawaii, the golden arches and the McDonald's flag have become almost as symbolic of American influence in 29 countries as the American flag and the hot dog. Ooops. Make that as American as McDonald's hot apple pie.

Ronald McDonald is the personality developed to attract the younger customers.

While expanding the number of restaurants throughout the United States and other nations, founder Ray Kroc insisted on keeping the menu small. Additions, such as the pies, Egg McMuffins and other items came very slowly. Mr. Kroc knew that he wanted to build a lot of restaurants, so that people would become familiar with McDonald's food and fast service. That way, they could go from town to town and know what they were getting. But he knew also that by offering only hamburgers and French fries and beverages (and later adding only a few things to that menu) he could maintain consistency in quality. He wanted no big surprises for the customers at McDonald's restaurants.

But of course Mr. Kroc knew he had to train cooks for the many McDonald's. So in 1961 he started up Hamburger University in the basement of the McDonald's in Elk Grove Village, which is just outside of Chicago. Learning how to "do it all" for customers, they flipped hamburgers and sizzled French fries until they got it just right.

And, just as modern day schools have now outgrown their little red schoolhouse days, Hamburger U. is now a three-story building with rooms full of equipment, where McDonald's managers come from all over the world to learn how to use the equipment and how to manage the busy restaurants, which can have thousands of customers a day.

Hamburger U. has become so sophisticated a school that cooking is no longer taught there. Students already learn that at one of the many regional schools. What they are learning at the U. is assembly line production of the food and how to get all teenagers (most of their employees are teenagers) to work while wearing that all-American smile. (Make that all-Japanese, all-European, all-Canadian—for many McDonald students are from the restaurants in foreign countries.)

A student at Hamburger U. practicing techniques she will use when serving the public.

This world-wide network is Mr. Kroc's dream. Now close to 80 years old and worth more than a billion dollars, he hadn't even opened a McDonald's restaurant until he was 52 years old. That was more than twenty-five years ago.

When Ray Kroc was a child, his mother gave him piano lessons to fall back on." Later, he tried piano playing to support his young family, even getting himself in trouble once in Florida for playing in an illegal bar during Prohibition. After that, he returned to Chicago, and began his career as a paper cup salesman. He also sold milk shake makers. Then, while on a trip to San Bernardino, California, he visited a drive-in restaurant that impressed him with its long, but fast-moving, lines of customers. For hours, he sat in his car in the parking area, watching people go in and out. Then, he got out of his car and into line to buy the only three food items the restaurant sold—hamburgers, milk shakes and the best French fries he'd ever tasted. He saw a simple food-processing method that set his mind in motion; they had several milk shake makers going at once, so that they could have lots of shakes ready at a time. Most restaurants made them one at a time. This restaurant was "mass producing" food, much the same way Henry Ford made cars.

He introduced himself to the owners, Mac and Dick McDonald. Eventually the three of them signed a contract. Mr. Kroc would build other restaurants, copying the food and the simple building style of this, the very first McDonald's restaurant. Mr. Kroc had his own ideas on making improvements, but they would come later.

One problem he did not foresee when he signed the contract was that some building modifications were going to have to be made. The contract had specified how each McDonald's restaurant should be built, down to which end the counter was on and which end had doors. But there was nothing in the contract telling where the furnace went—because the original restaurant in California hadn't needed one. In Illinois, they'd be serving nothing but frozen French fries. But finally, after a lot of legal wrangling, the first franchise restaurant was built in Des Plaines in 1955—furnace and all.

There were other setbacks along the way. At first, he was cautious about introducing new foods, but when Burger Kings, Arby's and Arthur Treachers started popping up near the signs of the golden arches, he started adding foods to compete. While the hash browns and sausage and eggs were a hit with the early morning crowd, other experimental things didn't make it. Mr. Kroc's own concoction—the hulaburger, a sandwich topped with pineapple, was a dismal failure.

But the rest is mostly a success story, and not just in food. Mr. Kroc's restaurants became so mammoth, they seemed to require a special "personality." Enter Ronald McDonald. There's only one Ronald on the television commercials, but thousands of others do appear at functions around the country. They gather for Ronald McDonald conventions each year in Chicago. There are hundreds of Ronald McDonald "houses" around the nation, too, where parents of sick children can stay while visiting the hospital.

Ronald has acquired quite a following. Said Hamburger U. teacher Tom Watson, "Among children, Ronald McDonald is the second most-recognized personality in the United States—after Santa Claus."

A businessman all the way, Mr. Kroc expresses his beliefs about becoming a millionaire in his book, "Grinding It Out—the Making of McDonald's."

"I speak of faith in McDonald's as if it were a religion. I believe in God, family and McDonald's—and in the office, that order is reversed." ■

HEAD-MAN IN THE HAIR-WORLD

By Phyllis I. Rosenteur

Paul Bergmann has his wigs displayed in almost all the Guinness museums here and abroad. Editors Norris McWhirter (left) and David Boehm are making sure it measures up.

Some people are born into the "Guinness Book of World Records," most get enrolled as the result of enormous effort, but Wig-Maker Paul Bergmann is probably the only person who achieved the honor by sheer accident. Comfortably, if inelegantly, located in an old loft building on the seedy West Side of New York City—far removed from the chic fashion world that he services—he recalled the phone conversation "that made me famous."

"Five years ago," he remembered, "someone from Guinness asked to speak to me. Strictly business...about the new Exhibit Hall about to open in the Empire State Building. Could I reproduce the record-holding wig? Well, of course I could—after all, the

Bergmanns have been in the business since 1873—but the caller seemed a bit skeptical. 'It's eight-feet long,' he warned me. When I said that wasn't much of a problem since I'd already made a wig *fifteen* feet long, I heard sort of a strangled sound. Apparently I'd just killed off the old record."

The fifteen-foot wig had originally been published in *Vogue* magazine, and on verification of the facts, Guinness promptly commissioned Paul Bergmann to re-create the incredible ebony-colored wig for the Exhibit Hall. Impressed with his artistry, Guinness also engaged him to reproduce the world's longest beard and moustache, both of which are still startlingly on display in the Exhibit Hall.

With no pun at all intended, Paul

Bergmann can truly be titled *Head-Man in the Hair-Line*. As President of Marco Bergmann Co. Inc.—the fourth generation of his family to hold that position, and so heir to 108 years' worth of experience—he can personally produce anything from a hair-net so fine as to be invisible an inch away—to the wildest, most eye-popping wig ever woven. The most spectacular would be the one in which he combined thirty blazing, neon-bright colors, none even close to a natural hair hue. Exuberantly artificial, it made the "fun wig" a lasting fashion.

When he hears "new," however, in connection with a hairpiece, no matter how odd its size, shape or substance, Bergmann tends to smile and shrug. There's nothing really new, he insisted...merely variations, many of his own invention, of the wiglets, falls, chignons, switches, braids, bangs, curls, queues, ringlets, rats, twists and toupées which every age or culture adapts to its own esthetic standards. In this, the Jet Era, the pace of the change has simply accelerated, he stated. Fads come and go so fast, nothing, including a wig, ever *wears* out. Instead, it's usually *thrown* out.

Some wigs, he admitted, *deserve* dumping, specifically the synthetic hairpieces of the 50's and 60's, made of highly inflammable fiber. The flameproofing applied at the factory, he informed us, undoubtedly went down the drain with the suds of the first shampoo. If you're still wearing one, he cautioned, one flick of a hot ash could turn you into a fiery redhead—for real!

Before chemistry evolved the silky, safe and shape-retentive fibers of today, the best craftsmen employed only human hair. At the time Paul's great-grandfather built his first factory in Laupheim, Germany, much of the raw material was provided by women who earned pin-money by the careful accumulation of daily "combings." More, though, came from small, poverty-stricken villages, principally in southern Europe, where hair was commonly considered a "crop," to be grown long, cut short, and sold. Bergmann theorizes that the kerchief worn by practically all peasant women was adopted as an easy, inexpensive way to conceal the "shame" of their short stubble. Then, as now, hair loss was highly traumatic.

Martha Swope

The "mane" challenge: Rising to the occasion, Paul Bergmann created this show-stopping wig for the Broadway hit "The Wiz."

During World War II, the last massive processing of human hair took place in the Bergmann plant, which had been appropriated by the Nazi state. Hitler's death camps supplied the hair! The German factory, completely rebuilt and back in the hands of the Bergmann family—some of them survivors of those camps—currently employs 150, who work almost exclusively with synthetic fiber.

Paul, who had fled from Germany before the Holocaust, was one of the first in America to experiment with artificial filaments and with other Occidental hair. "Even in this area, there was some discrimination," he explained. Until he perfected a superior "refining" system, Oriental hair was considered far too coarse and inferior for fine wigs, but by chemically burning off sharp barbs that form the outer sheath of each strand, he could achieve any desired *denier* or degree of softness. On the negative side, the more of the rough scales he stripped, the more fragile and costly the final product became. At least four ounces out of every pound of hair was lost in the process. "But the end result is worth it," he insisted. "In hairpieces, especially, the best is always the most expensive and, unfortunately, also least durable."

He winces when he sees a woman "heft" a wig. "And every one does...I suppose the heavier *it* feels, the more *she* feels she gets for the money. Now Charles Boyer knew better," Paul said admiringly. "He wore the airiest, most ethereal toupees I ever saw—so

delicate a breath could blow them away.

Since few individuals can afford what he now prefers to produce, Bergmann today leaves the mass market to others, and deals primarily with the extraordinary for "name" designers, stage productions, and special promotions of every sort. Although the firm still makes hairpieces for beauty parlors, as well as department, variety and chain stores, to sell under their special labels, as an individual he enjoys more of a challenge than the average wig offers.

One of his proudest achievements, for example, was the introduction of quality wigs for black women. In the exotic category, he created the lion's mane and topknot worn in *The Wiz*, and the spectacular "fall" that literally swept the stage in Broadway's *Timbuctu*. Among the oddities are the "weft pieces"—like lengths of shaggy yard goods in dire need of a shave—which are cut and sewn into ape suits.

Santa Claus wigs and whiskers are such a staple, he considered them hardly intriguing enough to mention, except to say that "before synthetics, the only way to get a good white was with a mix of yak hair and angora." One animal led to another, and to a memory that caused him to grin like a kid.

The German factory, he recalled, was commissioned by Haile Selassie, the "Lion of Judah," to make helmet-bushes and epaulets for the army of Ethiopia—strictly lions'-hair, which Ethiopia would supply, needless to say. However, the quantity Selassie provided proved to be insufficient, and what Selassie never knew was that his proud warriors were sporting lion hair *und ersatz*. But only the best of synthetics, Paul hastened to add.

In closing, Paul Bergmann has some words of advice for those who prefer their own home-grown hair to the most elegant *ersatz*. Not only can you keep what you have, but with patience, and a minimum outlay of money and effort, he claimed you can even replace some of what you lost. Concentrate on the scalp, he urged. Keep what hair you have clean and supple. Apply plain lanolin and massage deeply to stimulate the sebaceous glands and encourage new growth. Follow the regime faithfully, and in about three months, Paul Bergmann assured us, "you should feel the new fuzz!" ∎

Harpo Marx

Freud

Kissinger

Jan Leighton

JAN LEIGHTON

Guinness Interviewer Gets a Good Look at One Man—and a Thousand Faces

By Michele Voso

Not everyone gets a chance to have breakfast with Henry Kissinger or Fidel Castro, but I did. And if I had wanted to, I could have also met Issac Newton. Did I get some magic press card? One that not only allows entry anywhere today but any time in the past too? No, I didn't. I just had breakfast with Jan Leighton.

Who is Jan Leighton? You've probably seen him hundreds of times and never known it. In fact, it's possible that you could have seen him 1,800 times, and each time as someone other than himself. Jan holds a unique position in the "Guinness Book of World Records." His record is for the category "most roles played professionally by one actor," and it's not likely that there will be any contenders in line for his title.

Jan is unique: A person endowed with a seemingly supernatural talent to become almost any personality required by the director of a movie, commercial or ad. He has the uncanny ability to look just like the person he is portraying, without using any artifical "props," such as adding on a nose or prosthetically building up his cheeks or jaws. He

does it all—how? Not even Jan knows for sure.

Watching Jan become a character is as amazing as watching any metamorphosis in nature. He ducks into a hallway as Jan Leighton and reemerges as an old man, one of the phantom figures that might be gliding in and out of the alleys and streets of New York. His look has changed to one of glazed-eyed apathy—a hint of a stoop or was it a slight limp? It is the all-emcompassing image that he creates which draws you into believing he is that person/persona.

Jan's "Everyman" is exquisite. He plays an accountant better than an accountant, a butcher better than a butcher, Mr. Whipple better than Mr. Whipple.

The following incident on the set of a commercial with Mr. Whipple shows how even people who have been around when he is in costume sometimes get confused. Jan was dressed as Mr. Whipple and standing alongside him was the real Mr. Whipple. But Jan's moustache had become loose so he called for the

Clockwise: Van Gogh; Thoreau; Sherlock Holmes; Gen. Douglas MacArthur; Leonardo da Vinci; Lief Ericson; Thomas Jefferson; Christopher Columbus.

makeup man. The makeup man turned about to get the glue, turned around and walked back and pulled off the moustache—that is, tried to pull off the moustache. Resistance from the moustache and a loud yell from the real Mr. Whipple instantly made the makeup man aware of his mistake.

Sometimes Jan is so good he's too good. In 1973 Jan appeared as Bobby Riggs, the tennis player in a *New York Times* advertisement for an internationally known department store. The real Bobby Riggs saw the ad but couldn't remember posing for it. When he got in touch with the store they told him he was right, he had not posed for it—it was Jan Leighton looking like Bobby Riggs. Amusing? Of course, but not to Bobby Riggs. He brought a law suit against the store, which was settled out of court.

Jan also possesses a complementary talent. He has the ability to change his voice and is a master of foreign accents. A native of New York, Jan was hired to teach Jon Voight a Texas accent for his role in "Midnight Cowboy." He philosophically pointed out, "the only reason that I wasn't cast as Peter Falk's Italian mother in 'A Woman Under the Influence' was because John Cassavetes gave the part to his own mother." When he does his

Italian accent Jan claims "you can hear the bells of St. Peters."

Jan is constantly improving and adding to his vast repertoire of characters and replenishing his wardrobe. He is very particular about the details of his costumes and has spent over $600 for just the right coat to wear as Sherlock Holmes, and over $300 for the perfect Christopher Columbus spyglass. Rather than renting costumes, he found buying to be the only sure way of maintaining his standards.

Growing up during the Depression, Jan found character-acting in the park to be a good way to keep himself in candy and soda—but not quite the way you might expect. Portraying a youngster of less than average intelligence, he would tug so hard at the heartstrings of people passing by that they would loosen their pursestrings and come up with a nickel.

But he didn't realize the true scope of his talent until he got out of the armed forces after a stint as a pilot. He joined the Air Force because he was swept up by the romance of the life of a pilot and influenced by the dashing image Lindbergh made with his fur collar and strong, handsome face. He soon discovered that the "Lone Eagle" was a lonely bird and as far as Jan was concerned when you fly alone, there's no applause. ■

Left Column: Werewolf; Lincoln; Dracula; Groucho; Scrooge; Long John Silver; Charlie Chan; Popeye

Right Column: Ben Franklin; F.D.R.; Uncle Sam; Mark Twain; Edison; Napoleon; James Joyce; Terry Thomas.

MORRIS KATZ, WORLD'S MOST PROLIFIC PAINTER

By Charles Salzburg

Think of him, if you will, as the clone of McDonald's in the art world. He bills himself as "the world's fastest painter, creator of instant art," while some others (including the "Guinness Book of World Records") have dubbed him "the king of shlock art," and "a one-man art factory." Morris Katz could care less. Just so long as you spell his name right. Using only a palette knife and a roll of toilet paper to apply paint, he whips off a landscape oil in under 10 minutes ("3½ minutes is my record, and it's a painting of artistic merit"). What with going through nearly 9,000 rolls a year he almost single-handedly keeps a toilet paper factory in the black. "I use toilet paper as boldly as no man has ever used it before," he boasts, and who could dispute him?

A quick check of his "secret files" reveals that Katz, who uses between 600 and 800 gallons of oil paint a year, has, as of late 1981, compeleted the astronomical figure of 105,985 paintings. Undoubtedly, this makes him the most prolific painter in the world, beating Pablo Picasso, by a wide margin, and Katz is still going strong.

This Morris Katz, who at age 17 arrived in the United States 32 years ago from a D.P. camp in Germany, is involved in a self-declared "war of art," his weapons the knife and the toilet paper. But to further his cause, he's donned another role—that of entertainer. "Morris Katz, artist" (his New York City telephone-directory listing) is also a self-contained vaudeville act. Every weekend he leaves his West Village studio and art gallery ("The Amazing Randi lived here," he announces, hinting,

Michele Voss; painting on left, courtesy Cleon Jones

Morris Katz in his studio in Greenwich Village. Guinness staff member Gail Peterzell holds two paintings that were just completed in less than 5 minutes.

79

perhaps, that he Morris, is no less amazing) to take his show on the road.

Up to the Catskill mountains, where else? Kutschers, Browns, The Pines, the Nevele, the Concord—they welcome him with open arms. Once there, traveling in his van, Katz, *tummler* and artist, keeps the folks in stitches while he daubs away at canvas, Masonite, wood, glass, or anything else that's available.

One-liners like: "These are the highlights—you can tell because they're high up on the painting," keep them rolling in the aisles, begging for more.

"I run a comedy show," says Katz, who now flies all over the country with his act, "I make fun of myself. It's primitive humor, but they love it. They belch, they laugh, they buy. I

give them a fresh painting, like a fresh bagel."

At the post-show auction, they sometimes shell out as much as $125 per painting, while Morris hawks postcard reproductions of his work at a buck a pack. ("I lose money on them.")

Seated in his studio beside a glass tray of multi-colored oils, working on two paintings at one time ("for convenience, not for speed"), Katz recently told Guinness staff members of his life. He was born in 1932 in Poland. At 13 he studied under a German artist. "I always wanted to be a painter," he said. Nevertheless, after the war, while in the D.P. camp, he gained a diploma in carpentry, which he proudly displays, but he added, "toilet paper is my diploma in art." While talking, he mixed oils

with his palette knife and, using the edge, transferred paint to Masonite in bold strokes, forming trees and branches. For leaves, he daubed on color with his "art diploma," creating a rather representational painting in just a few minutes.

In 1949, he came here with a job in carpentry awaiting him. He also began selling art, painting in the conventional way—"in the style of the old masters. I had to make a living. I didn't have rich parents to support me. I didn't take handouts. I'm a highly independent man, and in order to be independent you must first survive."

He began showing in the Village, making $15 to $20 a week, while studying at the Art Students' League. "Soon, I decided I was really good enough—and compared to others,

Morris Katz on TV, getting ready to put the finishing touches on another Morris masterpiece.

Morris Katz travels all over the United States (and the world) demonstrating the technique that won him a place in the "Guinness Book of World Records."

---

excellent enough—to make my living as an artist. I spoke to older artists. They said, 'Katz, wait—you've got time. You're still young. You've got talent.' I didn't believe in talent. I believed in knowledge, which I had. I told them I was starting without their blessings. I was strong enough then to endure all the hardships I knew would come."

While doing research in 1956 for his unpublished *Dictionary of Color,* he developed his technique. "Mixing blobs of paint, I said to myself, 'Why not use the same palette knife to paint with?' So I did. The toilet paper came afterward. I ran out of rags. I used tissues, then toilet paper. Soon I picked up speed. If you know which way you're traveling, then you can run."

Making $65 a week, he hooked up with some furniture manufacturers. "Sometimes, so I heard, they even scratched my name off the painting and used a fancier name to get more money. After all, Katz is good for a delicatessen, not a painter. I got $6,

$8, $15 a piece, while they sold them for as high as $125."

So Katz got another brainstorm and eliminated the middleman. "My paintings can now be afforded by everybody. I mingle with the people. I'm not a snob. I don't believe in losing a sale." Today, he claims he's in the 50 percent tax bracket, while still keeping the price of his work down.

"When people meet me they say, 'You're Katz? The dealer told me you were an 85-year-old man, dying.' That's so they could get a higher price.

"Critics hate my guts. They say I prostitute myself. Not true. I believe in what I'm doing. I'm a pioneer in the art field. I'm an evangelist. I'm more popular at 49 than Picasso was at 49," he boasts.

And, at least in the Catskills, that seems to be the case. "After I finish my show, people come up to me and say, 'Your show made my weekend.' I combine comedy and creativity. People can see the creative process at

work. I inspire new artists. They watch me and learn. I've painted and sold more paintings than 100 artists in their lifetime."

What's on the horizon for Morris Katz? How about an autographed, broken-in palette knife? Or a benefit for "I Love New York"? ("I could leave New York and pay less tax, but I will not dump on New York now that I'm in the chips. I know my maker.") Or an original Katz going for $1,000? Why not? Now he's even breaking in his other hand to paint with ("This one gets tired"). And then there's the Katz Traveling Show. "If I got the right manager, I could make a fortune."

The interview is over, he offers a fresh painting—a black and white landscape. "Wait, I'll put in a house for you. You want a big one or a small one? Here, a small one. I'll put a person in the painting. It's you, running away from home. Wait— here, you're carrying a Katz painting. I'll put in another person. It's a butler waiting for you to return..." ■

YOUNGEST MILLIONAIRESS SHIRLEY TEMPLE FLUNKED "OUR GANG" FILM TEST

Shirley Temple was born April 23, 1928 in Santa Monica, California and became, according to the "Guinness Book of World Records," the youngest millionairess by accumulating wealth in excess of a million dollars before she was 10 years old.

While Shirley was the youngest to earn a million dollars, a number of other actors started young and some went on longer. For example, Mickey Rooney and Jackie Coogan started at age 6, Bebe Daniels at 7, Peter Lawford at 7 and Roddy McDowell at 8, Elizabeth Taylor at 10, Donald O'Connor at 11, Betty Grable at 13, Judy Garland at 14, and youngest of all were Natalie Wood at 5 and Anne Shirley at 4, if you don't count both Jackie Cooper and Liza Minelli who appeared in films as babies.

Shirley Temple's peak year was 1939 when she earned $307,014. She had risen to the top of the box office chart in 1935 at the age of 7, and remained there for the following three years with Will Rogers as her male counterpart in 1935, Clark Gable 1936-38, and Mickey Rooney in 1939. Who would have predicted such success after she had flunked a screen test for a role in the "Our Gang" comedy series before she got her start.

In recognition of her ability (and box-office appeal), Shirley was given a Special Award at the age of 6 by the Oscar committee for her "outstanding contribution to screen entertainment" in 1934. This made her the youngest winner of an Oscar for all time.

From the moment she was born, Shirley was given special attention by her mother. She was spared the childhood diseases from which most youngsters suffer. Like any other mother, Gertrude Temple sang and played the radio as she did her own housework. Shirley followed her around, acting out the music that was being played. She did little fun dance steps and showed herself to be a very graceful child. Her sense of rhythm and the pleasure she derived from moving about to music were clearly in evidence at a very early age.

When Shirley was 3, Mrs. Temple decided to send her to the Meglin dance school in Los Angeles. There a movie scout discovered her, although the exact circumstances are unclear. At any rate, 83 different people claim to have discovered her, but a man named Jack Hays did get her mother to sign a paper for Shirley to appear in a "Baby Burlesks" series at a rate of $10 per day including overtime. A check dated January 9, 1932 for the first day's work exists to prove it.

The comedies, spoofing first-run features, were backed by Universal Studios, and each took four days to make. Shirley appeared in eight of them, imitating Dolores Del Rio in the first, speaking French. In others she impersonated Louella Parsons as Lulu Parsnips, Marlene Dietrich as Moreles Sweettrick, La Belle Diaper, and a gold digger. Shirley was on her way, and the Meglin Kiddies School benefited from her success and publicity.

Her mother spent countless hours seeking the right parts for Shirley, and was not diverted from her goal by Harpo Marx, who was working at Paramount at the same time as Shirley was playing a small part in a western late in 1933. Harpo allegedly offered Mrs. Temple $50,000 to adopt Shirley. They never appeared in a film together.

Paramount let Shirley go after the western, and Fox Film Corporation did also after she had played in "Carolina" with Janet Gaynor, Lionel Barrymore and Robert Young. A short time later (still in 1934), Fox signed her again—this time for a musical after learning she could sing as well as dance. The film turned out to be *Stand Up and Cheer* and that was exactly what audiences did. Shirley was a big star.

This was the middle of the Depression and the film industry was excited about having a child star to take the public's mind off the hard times, and also away from the sexy scenes of Mae West movies, which were at that time being considered for censorship by Hollywood's Hays office.

Shirley's salary increased in leaps and bounds—from $75 to $150 per week. Paramount borrowed her for *Little Miss Marker* in 1934 at

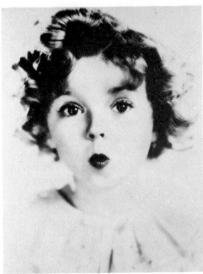

When Shirley Temple was the child star of the movies there was no doubt that she would make her fortune while young. To make a million in the 1930's was equivalent to making $14 million in 1982.

$1000 a week, and back at Fox she was raised to $1,250 a week. No American company would insure Shirley against accident, so Lloyd's of London wrote a policy in 1935 when she was 7, stipulating that the $25,000 benefit would not be paid if she met her death or was injured while drunk.

According to the Guinness book "Movie Facts and Feats," Shirley's mother made sure that she derived direct benefit from the style of Shirley's dresses, so when Fox sold manufacturing rights to Shirley's party dresses, it was Shirley who got the lion's share of the profits.

Shirley was also responsible for saving the Ideal Toy Corporation from a possible bankruptcy. Just at the right moment, Ideal bought the rights to portray Shirley in doll form, and every little girl in America had to have one.

By 1936, Shirley was receiving just over 60,000 letters a month, an all-time record for a mere human being. (Mickey Mouse was getting 66,000 a month). As age crept up on the golden-curled moppet, the mail dropped, and by the time she was 10, she had to give way at the top to Gene Autry, the popular guitar-strumming cowboy, although his 40,000 letters a month came nowhere near her best.

Shirley Temple was making fantastic amounts of money for her film studio and Uncle Sam, for a large portion of her half-million odd dollars a year in salary and endorsements had to be paid in taxes. As for Shirley's own pocket-book, her allowance was $4.25 per week.

The miniature Shirley Temple cottage built on the lot at Twentieth Century-Fox with its enclosed white fenced garden still stands, but it is used inside for offices, by necessity for very short executives.

When Shirley was 17 and her career almost at an end, she was engaged and later married to John Agar, but the marriage did not last. When she was 19, she played opposite Ronald Reagan in *That Hagen Girl,* and made her last film, *A Kiss for Corliss,* at the age 21 in 1949.

Now married to Charles Black, she served under President Eisenhower as the U.S. ambassador to Liberia, and unsuccessfully ran for Congress in 1967. Later she was appointed a member of the U.S. delegation to the U.N. General Assembly. ■

JUGGLERS' RECORDS HARD TO BEAT

Bobby May juggling 5 balls while doing a headstand on a table and rebounding the balls off a drum on the floor.

5 Clubs (For Time): Sergei Ignatov juggled 5 clubs for 16 minutes 20 seconds without fault in Russia, timed by his wife and witnessed by half a dozen perfomers.

7 Clubs: Three jugglers have been able to juggle 7 clubs in public: Albert Petrovski (in mid-1960's), Sorin Munteanu (1975), and Jack Bremlov (currently).

11 Rings: Three jugglers have juggled 11 rings in public: Albert Petrovski (1963-66) in the U.S. while he was on tour with the Moscow Circus, Eugene Belaur, and Sergei Ignatov (also on tour with the Moscow Circus.) Ignatov juggled each ring twice (22 throws) and finished by pulling each ring down over his head, one at a time.

10 Balls and 8 Plates: Enrico Rastelli of Italy, who was born in Russia and died in 1896, is the undisputed sole holder of these records.

5 Ping-Pong Balls: Gran Picaso in 1971 juggled the 5 balls with his mouth! It is believed that Picaso can do 6 ping-pong balls for a flash (each ball only once), but he has never performed this publicly.

6 "Frisbees": In his act with the circus, Gran Picaso has thrown out 6 with one hand and caught all 6 in the same hand when they return. Actually he does not use Frisbees, but small yellow plastic soup plates that respond like Frisbees.

"Cannonball" Juggling: Valeri Guryev juggled 3 balls weighing 26 lbs. each (a total of 78 lbs.) for a number of throws (not just a "flash") while on tour in the U.S. with the Moscow Circus.

Juggling while on a Unicycle: Freddy Zay once juggled 10 rings on a unicycle and regularly did 8. ■

No kidding. This is a Guinness correspondent (right) who is butting in to the editors' province suggesting we are unfair to goats.

CORRESPONDENT GETS OUR GOAT

Dear Guinness Book Editor:

I would like to know why the Guinness Book is ignoring that noble animal—the goat. Just one provocative line in "The Book" says that the goat has the hottest blood of any animal — including humans — 105.3°. You don't even say why. A statement like that is bound to arouse curiosity. It did mine.

What is to be said about goats? Just a few minutes spent in research has proven to me that when lists of fascinating animals are compiled, goats will be out front by a whisker. A few salient points you could cover?

1. How to get someone's goat and keep it...legally.
2. How to turn a Cashmere goat into a Cashmere coat.
3. Why goats eat books. (Ever since mine ate a "Guinness" paperback, he butts in on my assignments!)
4. The amazing difference between billies and nannies. (Goats are very sex-conscious, a fact I trust the "Guinness Book" to handle with its usual good taste.)
5. How Nubian goats got Roman noses.
6. Little known facts about a little known goat...the Toggenburg.
7. Will the craze for fine leather from goat skins endanger the species? (Who knows? Goats may become more precious than seals.)
8. Is it really true that old goats have more fun?
9. How about a list of kids of well-known goats who made it on their own?
10. Someone is always separating the sheep from the goats and the wheat from the chaff. (Are there any contests to see who can do this fastest?)
11. Why are goatees called goatees? Many other animals have chin whiskers. (Even some editors do, too.)
12. Then there's the bird, the goat-sucker, that becomes an udder fool around goats.
13. Scapegoats is a whole area that needs exploring. (Maybe we can get a comment from Nixon.)
14. Are all goats agile and able to climb mountains? (I'll bet some goats are klutzes.)
15. Capricorn is the zodiac sign of a goat. Are people born under this sign attracted to goats or attractive to goats? I am a Capricorn. (see picture).
16. Those Russian goats, the butt-in-skis, are a threat to other breeds, maybe to even other nations, and what is our government doing about it?

There's so much you could include in the Guinness Book on this adorable animal and you probably won't. On second thought I'll write a whole book about goats myself. Now I'll have to find a publisher who won't think I'm kidding!

Your faithful correspondent,
Adele Millard

THE GREAT AMERICAN FLAG

The greatest country in the world has to have the greatest flag. This idea does not emanate from the President of the United States, or for that matter from a general in the Army or from an admiral, as one might expect. Rather, it is the guiding inspiration of one loyal American, Len Silverfine, founder of the Great American Flag Fund, who single-handedly organized the building and raising of the world's largest flag.

The story about Len and his flag (or, as he is quick to point out, *our* flag) is the story of one man's dream and determination to restore the nation's sense of unity and the love that Americans once had for their country.

Len, like many Americans, feels that our national pride is rapidly being eroded and that the American consciousness is becoming self-directed. His dream is to unite all Americans by creating a non-political rallying point with a positive image and to rekindle respect for the symbol that once had the power to inspire us all.

The "Stars and Stripes Forever" is not just the name of a famous Sousa march, but what Len's flag looks like when it's on the ground. It covers an area of 86,378.5 square feet, is 210 feet 2 inches high and 411 feet wide. In everyday terms it is a flag that is a football field and a third in length. In a typical suburb, where each house is on a half-acre plot, you could fit four houses with front, back and side yards in the area this flag occupies. It weighs seven tons—one half ton more than the average weight of an African bull elephant (13,000 lbs.) which, according to the "Guinness Book of World Records," is the largest land mammal in the world. The stars, all 50 of them, are each 13 feet in diameter, and if you stack 10½ of our imaginary suburban homes one on top of the other, you will get an idea of how tall the flag is.

The stripes were all constructed from single strips of knit polyester, chosen for its superior strength, flexiblity and ability to stand up to continuous high winds as well as its resistance to the deteriorating effects of air pollution and sunlight.

Stars and stripes forever and ever and ever. Two acres of red, white and blue. Len Silverfine's helpers admire the fruit of their labor—all 7 tons of it. These volunteer helpers were able to unroll the mammoth flag faster and straighter than trained teams.

Other technical problems, besides the fabric choice, seemed insurmountable. The first flag that Len created in 1976 was raised on the Verrazano-Narrows Bridge (itself a one-time recordholder), which links Brooklyn to Staten Island at the entrance to New York Harbor. It hung for only eight hours before it was blown to shreds while Len and his crew of volunteers watched. It was a highly emotional time for all involved because many months of planning had gone into the project. But more than that, to Len it was symbolic of the deterioration of the fabric of American society.

In no time at all, Len began work on a second flag that was even bigger than the first. He's learned from his mistakes and, instead of using a sailmaker, he enlisted the help of an engineer, Herb Rothman. Herb was the chief engineer and one of the designers of the Verrazano-Narrows Bridge, which Len hoped to make the permanent home of the flag. Herb Rothman volunteered his services, time, and money, and, together with other volunteers, overcame all the problems of construction, storage, transportation, the mechanics of hanging, furling and unfurling the flag, and, of course, locating funds.

During a fund-raising tour, Len's enthusiasm and zeal attracted the attention of the Revlon Cosmetics and Fragrances Corporation's president, Paul Woolard, who gave Len the use of an office at their headquarters in New York, paid his expenses and made the first two major contributions. However, Len worked without salary from 1977 to 1980.

In spite of all the help from Revlon and other corporations, Len found himself in a tight situation on June 14, 1980—Flag Day.

He was to display the flag for the first time in front of the Washington Monument. He had counted on manpower from the various armed forces in helping to unroll the mammoth banner, a job that would take hundreds of strong men several hours to accomplish. But no military men could be obtained!

The flag had to be unrolled before 11 a.m. He had only a few hours to go and the prospects of having the flag set out in time for the ceremonies became dimmer and dimmer.

Flag Day in Washington, D.C. is a big event. People come from all parts of the country to celebrate and watch the parades. Hundreds of people already had assembled on the green near the Washington Monument— hundreds of people just waiting for the show to start. Why couldn't these people, Len thought, be his helpers instead of being spectators? Here was plenty of people-power, just what he needed, right where he needed it. He grabbed his megaphone and made an announcement to the crowd, explaining the predicament.

Within moments, hundreds of people were shedding their shoes and grabbing a section of the flag. Hundreds of people lined up alongside the rolled-up flag. They pulled, tugged, sweated and yelled. They laughed and moaned and helped each other and finally finished. Trained men, working under ideal conditions and with a knowledge of the situation, do not always roll without a wrinkle the first time, but that's just what Len's corp of volunteers accomplished. They did it right, and they did it in time.

The flag looked so beautiful on the green lawn with the monument behind it that Guinness decided to use the scene as the front cover photo for the 1982 edition of the "Guinness Book of World Records."

Here was Len's dream come true— Americans helping each other and working together. This was not all. Even Len was unprepared for what was the most moving moment of his odyssey with the flag.

Few people in America were undisturbed by the blow to our national pride dealt by the Iranians when they captured our people and held them hostage. When the hostages' release was imminent, Len lost no time in securing permission to display the flag at Andrews Air Force Base. He could think of no more appropriate symbol of welcome for our returning hostages.

In the predawn dark, before the arrival of the ex-hostages, the men of the Ironworker's Union and the American Legion worked up to their ankles in cold mud to ready the flag for the hostages' landing.

When dawn broke, the flag was ready. But tension began to mount when the hostages were delayed.

Hours of waiting ensued. Len and his volunteers finally spotted the aircraft bearing the freed hostages. The plane passed over the flag as it began its descent. Then the plane started to climb again! It gained altitude and passed over the flag a second time.

When the hostages had last seen the American flag it was in flames, burned in front of the American embassy by Iranian students. And now, as their plane prepared to touch down on American soil, they had asked the pilot to delay their long-awaited landing so that all of them could view for a second time that unbelievable moving sight of their flag, the biggest flag the world has ever seen. ∎

The Great American Flag—bigger and better than ever.

"GREASE," BROADWAY LONG-RUNNING MUSICAL, SETS WORLD RECORD

Broadway's longest running musical, "Grease," produced by Kenneth Waissman and Maxine Fox, ran eight years and became the longest running show in the history of the American Broadway theatre on the evening of December 8, 1979, passing "Fiddler on the Roof" when it played its 3,243rd performance.

"Grease"—a happy and tuneful tribute to the Fifties, which has been hailed by both critics and theatregoers alike, has spawned many film stars such as John Travolta, Barry Bostwick, Richard Gere, Jeff Conaway, Adrienne Barbeau, Marilu Henner and Treat Williams.

"Grease" was like an oak tree with spreading branches. It grew from a little acorn into a Guinness World Record. The acorn was a small show-case production with an amateur cast, playing in the basement of a converted trolley barn in Chicago, called the Kingston Mines Theatre. The show, more of a play at that time than a musical, filled the 150-seat house each weekend for about eight months.

Hearing of this more or less underground phenomenon, Broadway producer Kenneth Waissman and his wife, Maxine Fox, came out from New York to see the show and fell in love with the idea of making this reflection of teenage life of the late 1950's into a Broadway musical.

Under their guidance the two authors, Jim Jacobs and Warren Casey, moved to New York where they completely re-wrote the show, trimming the book and augmenting what little score there was. The producers then hired choreographer Patricia Birch to stage the musical numbers and Tom Moore, a young director. Over 2,000 young actors and actresses were auditioned to find

In "Grease" these young girls are singing "Freddy, My Love" at a pajama party. The musical is a glorification of the Fifties in rock 'n' roll.

the 16 performers who would make up the original Broadway cast.

On February 14, 1972, "Grease" opened at the Eden Theatre, a Broadway size house on lower Second Avenue, where other long-running entertainments had opened.

After "Grease" had 7 Tony nominations and enormous enthusiasm from the public, a move up to the Broadway mainstream was the only answer. In just four short months the deal was made to move "Grease" uptown, first to the Broadhurst Theatre and then to the Royale.

"Grease," which is named for the heavy oil boys used to plaster their hair with in the Fifties, was called "Vaselino" when it played in Mexico City, and if the show ever opens in France it may be titled "Brilliantine." But this, a musical tribute to the Fabulous Fifties, is as all-American as the memories it evokes of hot rods, pajama parties and high school proms. Along with the war-baby

generation that actually rocked and rolled its way through the Fifties, enchanted theatregoers of all ages are responsible for "Grease's" position at the top of the list of longest-running Broadway shows.

When it first premiered in 1972, few critics predicted prosperity for glorification of a decade that was both unstylish (bobby sox and bee-hive hair-dos) and unstable (the Korean War and the McCarthy era). Nevertheless, "Grease" became the inspiration for a Fifties craze.

"It was a time of prosperity and self-confidence in the country," co-author Jim Jacobs says. "We were out of the Korean War and hadn't yet got tangled in Vietnam. We had that nice, lovable, fatherly Ike in the White House. It was a time of normalcy and calm, that people now are craving to recapture after the turbulence of the Sixties and Seventies and the uncertainties of today."

Set in or near the hallowed halls of

fictional Rydell High, "Grease" confronts such ritualistic teen-age exercises as the chewing of bubble gum, piercing ear lobes, stealing hub caps and discovering sex. But the loosely structured plot is merely a point of departure for the rock'n'roll expression of adolescent agonies told in songs like "Alone at a Drive-In" and "It's Raining on Prom Night."

In one of the big production numbers, "Born to Hand-Jive," the authors have combined the "Hully-Gully" beat, the "Stroll" melody and the rhythm of the original "Hand Jive" to form a new/old song. This blending of different musical themes from the period is used throughout the show in order to provide a complete cross-section of Fifties music.

"Grease" was responsible for the resurgence of interest in rock 'n' roll. Today, it's hard to visit any city in the country and not find at least one radio station playing golden oldies.

"Grease," as a contemporary song recalls, is "a return to a simpler place in time," a time of sho-bop-be-bop, ballads of young love and High School Sock Hops; a fun, high-spirited musical romp back to the nifty Fifties.

The first "Grease" "find" to be tapped for TV stardom was Adrienne Barbeau, who originated the role of Rizzo—the tough leader of the Pink Ladies' gang in the very first Broadway production. Miss Barbeau soon became known to millions of TV fans as Bea Arthur's daughter, Carol, on the "Maude" series. She has also been a frequent guest with Johnny Carson.

"Adrienne had been knocking around quite a bit" says co-producer Maxine Fox. "She was doing off-off Broadway and even appearing as a go-go dancer in New Jersey. When she came to audition, we were impressed, but to make sure we made her audition four more times in competition with several other candidates."

TV-producer Norman Lear attended a performance of "Grease" one evening and was so taken with the young actress, he immediately offered her a screen test. Later, he signed her for the role on the now famous "Maude" show.

The most sensational example of the kind of success "Grease" has spawned is John Travolta. "John showed up one day at the auditions for our National Touring Company," explains Ken Waissman. "His only experience at the time had been

Some of the stars from "Grease" went on to movie roles—Jeff Conaway (center), John Travolta (lower right), Marilu Henner and Judy Kaye. James Dean's picture is in the background.

GUINNESS recognized the record set by "Grease" on December 8, 1979 when Geri Martin of the Guinness staff presented a certificate to Ken Waissman, producer of the show, at the Royale Theatre.

"GREASE" ran 3,388 performances (1972-1980) beating "Fiddler on the Roof's" record of 3,242 times. Here Barry Bostwick (on counter at right) leads in the show-stopping dance number "All Chocked Up" as Adrienne Barbeau (second from left) does her thing. (Right) John Travolta first made a name for himself in "Grease," along with a score of other youngsters. Ray De Mattis joins John in this number.

some summer stock work in New Jersey his home state. But we recognized his unique qualities and superior acting talent and cast him in the role of 'Doody' a shy adolescent who is in love with his guitar. He was wonderful in the part and we kept him on the road for a year."

Following that, Waissman and Fox brought Travolta to New York where he played the same role in the Broadway company. Then they gave him a featured part in their new musical "Over Here." Some TV scouts heard his voice on the cast album and came to see him in the show," continues Miss Fox. "After his contract with us was over, they signed him for 'Welcome Back, Kotter,' and after that the enormously successful "Saturday Night Fever." Travolta, of course, hit a second peak in his career in the movie version of "Grease," which became the most successful musical picture of all time, grossing $93,292,000, right behind "Star Wars" and "Jaws" in all-time box office receipts.

Richard Gere, of "Grease" fame, who later played Diane Keaton's boyfriend in "Looking for Mr. Goodbar," also starred in "Blood Brother."

Tony Award winner Barry Bostwick went on to star with George C. Scott in the film "Movie, Movie." ∎

(Below) In the school gym, the ladies of "Grease" come back to school and sing about their boy friends and summer romances in this "Summer Nights" number.

J.P. MORGAN, WORLD'S WEALTHIEST MAN LIVED IN NON-INFLATION TIMES 100 YEARS AGO

Although today there is only one living billionaire, Daniel K. Ludwig, and his fortune until most recently was estimated at $3,000 million, this wealth could not compare with that of John Pierpont Morgan, father and son, who had fewer dollars perhaps but lived in non-inflationary days, late in the 19th and early in the 20th centuries.

Morgan (1837-1913) was an international private banker who created a vast financial and industrial empire without parallel in American history. He was so rich that twice, in 1895 and again in 1907, he saved the United States government from insolvency. In 1895, in the depths of a depression acting with the approval of President Grover Cleveland, he acquired more then $65,000,000 in gold for the U.S. government (and millions for himself!) saving the Treasury Department from having to default on redeeming its currency in coins. Then, in 1907, he mobilized the banking strength of New York to avert widespread collapse following a Wall Street panic. As a result, besides making millions for himself, the House of Morgan gained tremendous influence in the business world—in railroads, steel, everything.

Influential in Britain too, J.P. Morgan spent generously for art masterpieces in Europe. Under the guidance of art connoisseurs like Lord Duveen, he became the "biggest and most dominating figure in an art-buying bonanza," according to the Guinness book, "Art Facts and

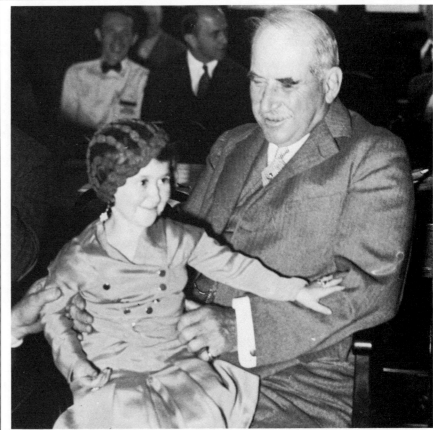

When the Senate was investigating Wall Street in 1933 after the stock market crash, the son of J.P. Morgan, the world's wealthiest man of his time (1867-1943), was the star witness. While he was testifying, a lady midget came out of nowhere and jumped up into his lap while cameras clicked. Morgan was amused.

Feats." He bought art collections as avidly as he did ships or railways. In about 20 years he spent $60,000,000 on objects that have since gone to enrich public collections in America, notably the Metropolitan Museum of Art in New York. Also the Morgan Library in New York became the repository of his illumin-ated manuscripts and books. J.P. gave generously to hospitals and schools, although he was denounced by the press and some of the public for his power and influence in business and politics. To control banking practices, the Federal Reserve System was established in 1913, to control Morgan's "money trust." ∎

FIRST GUINNESS AWARD HONORS BEATLE PAUL McCARTNEY AS SONGWRITER SUPREME

Guinness Superlatives, British publishers of the Guinness Book, paid tribute with a unique award to Paul McCartney as the most honored composer and performer in music, at a special presentation ceremony held at Les Ambassadeurs, London, in October, 1979.

To commemorate the occasion, Norris McWhirter, the author of the Guinness Book, presented Paul McCartney with a unique disc, made of rhodium, one of the world's rarest precious metals. Rhodium is twice as valuable as platinum, with a market price of about $872 per ounce.

McCartney was honored especially for the unique achievement of having gained three entries in the world's fastest-selling copyrighted book. Born in Liverpool on June 18, 1942, and one of the four Beatles, McCartney holds records as:

1) THE MOST SUCCESSFUL COMPOSER OF ALL TIME: 43 songs written between 1962 and 1978 have each sold over one million copies.

2) A RECORD NUMBER OF GOLD DISCS: 42 with the Beatles, 20 with Wings and one with Billy Preston. Total: 63.

3) THE WORLD'S MOST SUCCESSFUL RECORDING ARTIST: Estimated record sales: 100 million albums, 100 million singles.

Norris McWhirter said prior to the presentation: "It has been our practice, over many years, to issue certificates to new world record holders. Having read in a newspaper article that Paul McCartney was one of the readers of our book, we thought of making a presentation to him to mark the fact that he is a Triple Superlative who has been featured in so many of our editions that we have

Paul McCartney (top left) in the early days of the Beatles is surrounded by Ringo Starr (top right), George Harrison (lower left) and the late John Lennon.

Capitol Records

come to regard him as a virtual fixture.

"Since, in the field of recorded music, gold and platinum discs are standard presentations by record companies, we felt we should make a fittingly superlative presentation of the first ever rhodium disc with a special label listing his three achievements."

America was represented at the ceremony by Paul's wife, Linda Eastman McCartney of the American family that founded Kodak, and by Lincoln A. Boehm of the American Guinness Book staff.

Today, McCartney is regarded as the most accomplished figure in popular music. His superlative achievements include records for both performance and composition, a coupling of skills not frequently found in the great popular artists of this century.

McCartney has the unique distinction of being a part of the most successful group of all time, the Beatles, and continuing to amass gold discs both on his own and with the group Wings.

The Beatles (George Harrison, the late John Lennon, Paul McCartney and Ringo Starr) first got on the best-seller chart in Britain with "Love Me Do" on October 11, 1962, and peaked at number 17. "Please Please Me," released in the first month of 1963, did much better, getting to number 2 on the official chart and number 1 in several others.

"From Me to You," the next single began a string of eleven number ones. No artist has approached this accomplishment. The Beatles held the number 1 position for sixteen weeks in 1963 alone, the most weeks any British artist has topped the United Kingdom singles chart during a calendar year. "She Loves You," the follow-up to "From Me to You," became the best-selling 45 rpm record in British history, selling over one and a half million copies in the U.K. alone.

"I Want to Hold Your Hand," the next single, began the Beatles' invasion of the United States.

It was the first of their twenty American number ones, more chart-toppers than any other artist has accumulated. In Britain, their seventeen number-one hits were equalled, though not surpassed, by the late American singer Elvis Presley. "I Want to Hold Your Hand" remains the top-selling British disc of all time, having achieved global sales in excess of 13,000,000.

In April, 1964, the Beatles held the top five positions on the Billboard Hot 100, the definitive American singles chart. The titles were, in descending order: "Can't Buy Me Love," "Twist and Shout," "She Loves You," "I Want to Hold Your Hand" and "Please Please Me." No act has duplicated this domination of the singles market.

The Beatles also broke all sales records with their albums. "Meet the Beatles," the re-titled British album "With the Beatles," became the best-selling American album. Its success revolutionized the long-playing record market, making rock music the predominant force in the field for the first time. The Beatles established the still-standing U.K. record for advance sales of an album with 750,000 orders for the late 1964 release "Beatles for Sale." By the end of 1977 estimated sales of the group's recorded work was 100 million singles and 100 million albums, a double that remains unmatched. The group had earned 43 gold discs.

Paul and Linda McCartney are joined by Norris McWhirter, Editor of the Guinness Book, for the presentation of the first ever rhodium disc, honoring the ex-Beatle's triple listing in the Guinness Book of World Records.

One of the songs Paul McCartney wrote for the Beatles, "Yesterday," is the most recorded song in history, having been recorded in over 1,200 versions. Paul's song "Michelle" won the American Grammy for the Best Song of 1966; the same year he won another Grammy for the Best Song of 1966; in the same year he won another Grammy award for the Best Contemporary Solo Vocal Performance, "Eleanor Rigby." The Beatles album "Sergeant Pepper's Lonely Hearts Club Band" won the Grammy award for the Best Album of 1967, and a poll of international rock critics ten years later named it the best rock LP ever.

The world realized the Beatles had disbanded when Paul's first solo album "McCartney" was released in the spring of 1970. Made with the assistance of his wife, Linda, it became his first post-Beatle American number one.

It included the now classic "Maybe I'm Amazed," which was used to great effect in the hit 1978 film "An Unmarried Woman." Paul and Linda's duet LP "Ram" and single "Uncle Albert/Admiral Halsey" both reached number one on the respective U.S. charts in 1971.

Later that year McCartney formed the group Wings, whose fluctuating membership has always included Linda and guitarist Denny Laine. They scored a double number one in America in 1973 with the single "My Love" and the album "Red Rose Speedway."

"My Love" was followed by Paul's theme for the James Bond film "Live and Let Die," an international top ten hit that earned the writer an Oscar nomination. "Band on the Run," which was another 1973 release, contained three U.S. top ten hits, and every time one of those singles peaked, the album went to number one. It was the first album to top the American chart on three separate occasions.

"Band on the Run" proved to be another American number one single for Wings. The first release from the gold album "Venus and Mars," "Listen to What the Man Said," also reached the top of the Hot 100 and gave the Wings group a streak of eight consecutive American top ten singles, the longest string going at the time. "Silly Love Songs" and "With a Little Luck" have since reached number one in America, with "Silly Love Songs" Billboard's top single of 1976.

Even these feats were dwarfed by the success at home of "Mull of Kintyre," the Christmas 1977 smash. It was the first British hit to sell over two million copies and replace "She Loves You" as the U.K.'s all-time number one record, a position it has retained despite several recent challenges. In addition, "Mull of Kintyre" remained nine weeks at number one. No record in the rock era has exceeded this run.

In 1979 Paul McCartney earned further gold discs for the single "Goodnight Tonight" and the album "Back to the Egg."

For the past fifteen years, critic Paul Gambaccini has pointed out, Paul McCartney has entered both the British chart and the American top 40. This achievement over such a period of time is unmatched. ■

SHHHHH!

We're in the quietest place on earth and we're just a few miles from the heart of New York City.

It's hard to believe that any place so close to such a noisy part of the world could exist. But it *does* exist and it has been recorded in the "Guinness Book of World Records" for many years in the chapter on Science.

Bell Labs is the home of the quietest spot. Built as a 210-acre complex in Murray Hill, New Jersey, is Bell Telephone's research facility. There you will find a room called the "Anachoic Chamber" or "dead" room. What use is a "dead" room? Bell Labs finds it indispensible in developing techniques to improve the sound of your favorite recordings with near perfect fidelity, perfect the sound and clarity of an artificial larynx to aid people with speech impairments due to accident or disease, or help NASA develop techniques for space programs.

What's it like in the "dead" room? Well, the word quiet takes on a completely new meaning. Sound is completely absorbed. Any words you utter are "gobbled up" almost before they leave your mouth.

Its physical characteristics are best described as two rooms, one on top of the other. However, instead of a floor/ceiling separating the two levels, there is only a metal grid that springs up and down slightly when you walk on it. Not only are you not on a solid surface but you are also in semi-darkness, which adds greatly to the strangeness of being in the room

Fiberglass wedges extend 5 feet

The "dead" room at Bell Labs in Murray Hill, N.J. Note that the man is standing on a grid. The floor is not mirroring the walls.

from all six surfaces: walls, ceiling and floor absorb 99.9 percent of any audible sound made. Behind the fiberglass is 24 inches of masonry

blocking out the noise from outside the room. The effect is eerie.

You might think that the lack of sound is a pleasant experience. What

94

Two people and a split-head employed by Bell Labs listen to the Jupiter Symphony by Mozart in an experiment conducted by Dr. Manfred Schroeder to determine the best acoustic characteristics of concert halls. The results will be used to improve existing concert halls with demonstrated acoustical problems and build better ones in the future.

could be better than a place to escape from 99.9 percent of unpleasant sounds that are a natural part of city living? It's not. It's too much of a good thing!

After only a few minutes in the "dead" room you begin to *hear* sounds. Your own sounds! Rushing blood, throbbing arteries expanding and deflating lungs. If you heard these sounds all the time it would probably affect your sanity. When you start to hear the pounding of your pulse and your stomach while digesting lunch, it's time to leave.

The "dead" room is just an interesting little corner of the Bell Labs facilities.

The invention of the telephone in 1876 by Alexander Graham Bell precipitated the multi-billion-dollar AT&T empire and helped create an explosion in space-age technology which has had an impact on almost every aspect of our lives.

An article with a more technical slant would include words such as: epitaxial transistors, Klystrons, magnetic bubbles, picosecond switching, quantum wells and more, but there are some items to which a layman can more easily relate, such as: the Magnetron. This device was developed during World War II and was responsible for knocking down 76 percent of the German buzz bombs sent to England reappearing in, of all places, the kitchen of today as a component of the microwave oven.

In 1962 Telstar I was set in orbit and in 1963 Telstar II was launched, making coast-to-coast telephoning faster and cheaper by bouncing signals off the Echo Balloons that are on board these two satellites. With Bell Labs help, NASA was able to launch over 400 scientific space vehicles incorporating devices for gathering scientific information that will lead to further advances in communication.

Creative and efficient, Bell Labs has also found a way to even make use of the pauses in our telephone conversations. Called TASI (short for Time Assignment Speech Interpolation), it uses natural pauses in a speaker's conversation to transmit portions of other conversations, saving the caller money and making Ma Bell look very clever. ∎

THE CELESTIAL SUITE

See What You Get in The World's Most Expensive ($3,000-a-Night) Hotel

When the editors of the "Guinness Book of World Records" were informed that the price of the Celestial Suite at the Astro Village Hotel in Houston, Texas had been raised from $2,500 per night to $3,000, they thought the time had come to find out just what the world's most expensive hotel suite was like.

Armed with notepads and camera, two of them set off for Houston on a red-carpet ride on Eastern Airlines (a Guinness recordholder itself) to investigate.

The following is an account by Gail Peterzell and Michele Voso of their experience in the Celestial Suite.

* * *

"Would you like to sleep in the Tarzan and Jane room, or would you prefer Lady Chatterley's suite?"

Caught off guard, we stared at the desk clerk in slack-jawed amazement.

"I beg your pardon?"

"You're staying in the Celestial Suite this evening, right?"

"Right."

"I just wanted to know how many beds we should turn down for you."

"Oh. Well, maybe something a little less...stimulating, perhaps?"

Would we have hanging vines and trumpeting elephants stampeding through the room?

Guinness editors pride themselves on their unflappability in the face of the extraordinary. However, the Celestial Suite came very close to flapping us.

We decided to look before we leaped into any beds in this suite and set up a meeting place with a secret signal in case we became separated.

"Don't forget your keys," the desk clerk shouted as we moved toward the elevator. The keys in this case

The Tarzan room in the Adventurer Suite.

were a bundle of approximately 10 pounds in weight.

We split the keys among the three of us—our guide, Cassie joined us at this time and we proceeded to the private bubble elevator that services the suite.

We then thanked Cassie for her thoughtfulness and made arrangements to meet again in an hour for dinner.

Even without the Celestial Suite, the Astro Village Hotel is an exciting place to stay. Its big comfortable rooms and gourmet dining room make it a magnet for conventions.

We spent several very entertaining hours dining with Cassie and Nan Stone, the hotel's director of sales. Both Cassie and Nan regaled us with

stories and anecdotes of Texas and the Celestial Suite.

Our evening was ending and jet lag was taking its toll. We said goodnight and summoned our private elevator.

When we had left the suite to have dinner, the sun had just started to set and the rooms were still bright with its glow.

Now, all of a sudden, as we stepped out of the elevator, we became aware of the silence. Darkness hung around all the windows like thick black drapes. The echoing footsteps of the afternoon, a background noise to the chattering and laughing, sounded hollow and resonant as they bounced off all the marble and glass surfaces. The artificial sunlight that looked so

Guinness reporters Gail Peterzell (left) and Michele Voso taking a break in the Astro Village Mini-Dome.

cheery in the afternoon had lost its warmth.

We conversed in whispers.

"Why are you whispering?"

"I don't know. Why are you whispering?"

"I don't know either."

"Where do you want to sleep?"

"Where do *you* want to sleep?"

Shrugs.

* * *

The elevator runs on the outside of the hotel wall and is glassed in on all sides. Since the Astro Village is the highest building for miles around, we were treated to a panoramic view of Texas.

The doors opened on a foyer with marbel floors, fully furnished with antiques.

"Let's start with the Master Suite," our guide suggested.

It took us a few minutes, but we finally found the right key.

Cassie pushed open the double doors, grinning like the Cheshire Cat.

To the left and up a short flight of steps, was the most remarkable room either of us had ever seen. We didn't know which way to look first.

The bed was gigantic. It would easily hold 10 people. The ornately carved posts and headboard depicted Romans doing all sorts of things and arrested our attention for a while. Above the bed hung a thick red canopy. Steps led up and down to various nooks and crannies in the room. The mantle of the stone fireplace had been decked with fresh flowers.

Off to the far end of the room was the Roman Bath with a tub that could accommodate 10 or more people and hold 100 gallons of water. The touch of a hand turned on a dragon-headed waterspout that gurgled water into the ornate sink that was surmounted by an elaborately carved and gilded mirror. The shower area, off to the left, was built for 10 too.

We put down our pocketbooks and ran around turning on all the faucets.

"Does all this stuff really work? It looks like the set from a movie."

Cassie, delighted that the room had this effect on us, proceeded to tell us that the whole suite was designed by Mr. Harper Goff. We looked at each other and shrugged.

"Who's that?" we inquired.

"He was the Academy-Award-Winning set designer who created the sets for '20,000 Leagues under the Sea'."

Somehow that fit, we both agreed.

Back down the steps and through a door, we entered the Library.

The walls here were lined with bookshelves and a crystal chandelier hung from the high ceiling. Beautiful fresh long-stemmed roses were in vases placed around the room.

"Who's idea was this suite?"

"The Judge's," was the reply.

"What judges?"

"Not judges," giggled Cassie, "The Judge's. Judge Roy Hofheinz. He was the mayor of Houston at one time but of course he is better known, nationally, as the man who masterminded the Houston Astrodome."

Rich and powerful, The Judge, after completing the Astrodome and Astroworld and the Astro Village Hotel, decided he wanted to be close to his Astrodomain so he built the Celestial Suite on top of the completed hotel.

The Judge left his mark. The private viewing and meeting rooms in the Astrodome are very similar to the décor in the Celestial Suite. Got a fantasy? Pick a room.

Sleep in the Sadie Thompson, the Lillian Russell, P.T. Barnum or the Fu Manchu. Snack in the Monterey Kitchen with Spanish tile on the walls and floors and a wine cellar. (Well, not exactly a wine cellar since we were on the roof). Or dine in the Bird Cage dining room, with its control panel full of switches for adjusting the lighting to suit the mood of the occasion. The controls were not just for brightening or dimming the lights, but there was a choice of colors too—blue, yellow and red.

Bamboo furniture and a slow-turning ceiling fan carries out the theme in the Sadie Thompson. Lots of frills and lace in the Lillian Russell with its purple and white scheme.

The bathrooms in every suite have gigantic colored marble tubs and the sinks are adorned with faucets and spouts of swans or dragons or some kind of animal. In the Fu Manchu Suite, little brass Chinese men hold up the soap dishes and dispense the toilet tissue.

Are you wondering about what the Tarzan Room looked like? No elephant, fortunately, but split level, with vines hanging from the balcony, and full-size African statues were The Judge's choice for this suite.

"This room is a big hit with the kids," Cassie told us.

"The kids!" screamed Gail. "You'd waste a room like this on kids!"

"Did I hear someone mention Lady Chatterley?"

"Come this way," said Cassie.

Through a door and up a stairway we entered the Victorian world of Lady Chatterley. Overstuffed chairs and sofa and bent-wood furniture were featured in this suite. We were getting used to the monstrous beds by this time, but the lighting in Lady Chatterley's boudoir was the thing that set the tone here.

Not all the furniture in the suites were original antiques. When The Judge couldn't find an original piece, he was not above throwing in a fake to make sure that the mood of the room didn't suffer for want of props.

We were so wrapped up in running around looking at everything that we almost forgot to ask about former occupants of the suite. The list that Cassie rattled off naturally led us to speculating about what celebrity chose to sleep where.

"Muhammad Ali! He must have used the Master Suite."

"Jerry Lewis! The P.T. Barnum Suite, naturally."

"Lady Bird? The Bird Cage Dining Room?"

We went on like that for a while, covering Greer Garson, presidents and premiers of various countries and companies, June Carter and Johnny Cash.

A typical decoration in the Celestial Suite.

And then... "Lets go down the Lane of Lanterns to the other half of the suite," suggested Cassie.

"The other half?" we exclaimed.

The Lane of Lanterns is artificially lit, but it is done so cleverly that it looks like natural sunlight. The long hallway with its iron grillwork and lanterns looked like a street in New Orleans. Along the walls were pots of bright yellow chrysanthemums, that gave everything a fresh, outdoors feeling.

Giddy with anticipation, we set off for "the other half." The other half is nothing less than a ballroom—Judge Hofheinz style. Designed to look like a mini-version of the Astrodome, the Minidome had a dance floor that looked like a baseball field, a bar, dining room and a great view. A miniature replica of the famous Astrodome scoreboard was lit up that day with an Astro greeting:

"The Astro Village welcomes Gail and Michele" in bright lights flashed on as we entered the Minidome.

"It's too spookey in here. Let's look for another room."

"We went back to the Master Suite to get our things.

Off we went on our search to find a room a little less awesome to spend the night in.

"Look, you must have knocked over a flowerpot."

"I didn't knock it over. I thought you did."

The beds were turned down in the rooms, and wrapped chocolates were on the pillows. That solved the problem about the flowerpot. We deduced that the chambermaid must have tipped it over. We teased each other for being so susceptible to the movie-set atmosphere.

Nevertheless, we still turned on all the TV sets as we went in and out of the rooms, hoping to dispel some of the silence. We had to run around turning them all off again, though, because it was worse with muffled voices coming from all over the place.

The P.T. Barnum Suite was our choice, finally. It had a sitting room called The Big Top Room that had comfortable furniture, a ceiling light made of three red and white rings and three rings woven into the carpet below the light. Murals on the walls depicted the life of P.T. Barnum and circus greats like General Tom Thumb. Gilded masks of roaring lions decorated the doors and statues of pretty ladies were on pedestals on either end of the sofa. The Big Top Room and the Bandwagon (bedroom) Room were separated by a beautiful stained-glass door.

We ate our chocolates while we inspected the bed. If the bed in the Master Suite slept 10, then this bed must surely be comfortable in accommodating 15. It was made from an old circus bandwagon, repainted in gold and red with the wheels still attached. A huge gilded peacock served as the headboard, and a velvet sofa was at the foot end.

The day was over. Our strength was drained. Picture-taking and note-making left us little desire to go over the rooms again for details we might have missed on the first tour.

What little energy was left we needed for climbing into the bandwagon bed.

"Do you think I should check the wheels? I can't find the emergency brake," I asked, plumping up my pillows.

"I think you should go to sleep." ∎

MOTHER OF FATTEST TWINS (727 lbs. and 747 lbs.) RECOLLECTS THEIR BIRTH

Billy and Benny McGuire (né McCrary) weighed 727 and 747 lbs. respectively when this picture was taken. Eating didn't make them fat—it was a glandular problem.

The world's heaviest twins, Benny and Billy McCrary (who used the name McGuire when they became performers), were smaller than average babies at birth, their mother told the Guinness Book editors recently.

"Billy was 5 lbs. 5 oz. and Benny was 5 lbs. 3 oz. They seemed to be average weight until at 4½ years they had red measles. At Duke University Hospital, the doctors diagnosed their growing so fat as a glandular problem.

"By the time they were 9, they were about my weight—an average 340 lbs. (I'm now down to 105.) We never did anything special about their rooms or beds. They used to play tricks on me, like fooling me on the phones as their voices were very much alike.

"At 12 when they were in school, they weighed 410 to 430 lbs. and I knew they had a problem. Their dad only weighs 225 lbs. A thermostat inside their body had become unbalanced.

"The school and doctors suggested that they get manual outdoor work so we bought ourselves a farm, and the twins worked on it. They loved raising cattle, horses and doing rodeos."

That's how they got into the entertainment world, first wrestling and later just exhibiting themselves when they weighed 727 and 747 lbs. (Billy died in an accident in 1979.)

Mrs. McCrary never had any other children, and says "I never had any trouble with them, and every second of their life has been a pleasure to me.

"We are Christians and while Billy's death was a great shock to us, we expect we'll meet him someday." ■

STRUGGLES OF THE GIANTESSES

When Sandy Allen was born in Chicago on June 18, 1955, she weighed only 6½ lbs. but soon after birth she began growing faster than female babies usually grow.

The Allen family soon moved to the town of Shelbyville, Indiana, and her grandmother, with whom she lived, knew she had a rare person developing. By the time Sandy was in high school she towered over her classmates. By the time she was 15 she was well over 6 feet tall, and she had "the worst time of her life," she recalled in a conversation with the editors of the "Guinness Book." Her schoolmates' taunts spiked her during these high school days. This teasing became so bad, Sandy said "I wanted to drop out of school." But Sandy, with her strong will and determination, was not going to let her classmates ruin her life and so she started overcoming her many obstacles. In the meantime, a young brother was born of normal size.

Sandy learned to be a typist and got a job working for the State in Indianapolis. In this environment, too, her size made her outstanding and attracted more attention than she wanted. When she reached the height of 7 feet the newspapers in Shelbyville wrote her up as perhaps the tallest woman who ever lived.

A newspaper clipping was sent to the editors of the "Guinness Book" and it was verified that Sandy, who had now reached 7 feet 7¼ inches, was indeed the tallest living woman.

However, a woman who was born in England in 1895 had reached 7 feet 11 inches in height, but had died in 1922, and her measurement was estimated from a skeleton. This giantess, named Jane Bunford, was generally believed to be the tallest woman who ever lived. With the notoriety that Sandy got after being acclaimed the living record holder by Guinness, she was invited to appear on the David Frost TV show, where millions of

Sandy Allen at the Guinness Museum in Niagara Falls, Ontario.

Gordon Counsell, Inc.

people saw her. This opened the door to many talk shows both on TV and radio. The Italian movie director, Federico Fellini, was in the process of making a movie in Rome, and invited Sandy to appear in it. She was flown to Europe by Fellini and given a small role.

Getting into the "Guinness Book" was the best thing that has happened to Sandy. Old schoolmates who tormented her before are now proud to be seen with Sandy. "I can meet so many unusual and famous people although some people still point and stare at me. I feel they have the problem, not me."

By May 1976, the Guinness World Record Exhibit Hall was ready to open in the Empire State Building in New York City, and Sandy became the major attraction at the opening event. When she walked through the streets of New York near the Empire State Building on Fifth Avenue and 34th Street, crowds of 1,000 people and more followed her.

In New York, Sandy has appeared on many TV shows, most recently on the "Tomorrow" program with Tom Snyder. She shows great poise in her interviews with newspaper reporters, and had received the greatest publicity a giantess ever got.

In 1978 she was invited to the opening of the Guinness Museum in Niagara Falls, Canada, and so popular did she become that she was invited to be a permanent guest there. Under the management of Mac Howe, she makes trips to various events representing the various Guinness museums. She is still appearing at the Niagara Falls Museum and telling "tall tales."

Sandy reached her maximum height of 7 feet 7¼ inches at the age of 22 years and has to wear size 22 shoes. Far from being ashamed of her excessive height, Sandy is proud of it and wears T-shirts with sayings such as "How'd you get so short?" and "I enjoy short people—I just had three for lunch."

It was the malfunctioning of her pituitary gland that caused Sandy to grow so fast, and in July 1980 she underwent surgery on that gland to prevent further growth. Sandy's big problem is weight. Her legs and feet are burdened with quite an excessive amount of pressure and Sandy has difficulty walking. When interviewed for the Guinness Stories Book, Sandy said, "I enjoy being tall and I enjoy being the tallest woman in the world."

What will happen to Sandy Allen now that a young Chinese girl named Zeng Jinlian has grown to a height of 8 feet?

Sandy Allen will still be the tallest American woman of all time. She is not physically able to perform any other task than as a museum guide, and that is what she intends to do, as well as make tall people comfortable with their height.

As for Zeng Jinlian, she is 18 now and growing fast. In November 1980, she was 7 feet 10½ inches tall, and in May 1981, she had passed the 8-foot mark. Unable to stand erect even with help, she is easily tired and has diabetes which, however, is said not to be related to her size. But it should cause her to be careful of her diet. Eating a breakfast or lunch that includes 20 steamed rolls won't help her diabetes, nor will her consuming 6 big bowls of rice at each meal. Yet she must stock that 325-lb. figure.

Zeng Jinlian sleeps in a 9-foot bed in the same room with her mother, and lives a quiet type of life, close to her family of mother, father and three brothers.

Zeng is a great reader, we are told, so we are sending her a copy of this book. ■

By July 1981, Zeng Jinlian (pronounced San Chung Lin) reached 8 feet, becoming the first woman to reach such a height. Still growing, Zeng Jinlian, 18 years old, lives with her family in the Hunan Province in central China.   **Flash! She died in February, 1982.**

MEET DONG KINGMAN— THE FASTEST PEN IN THE EAST

by Peggy S. Boehm

To anyone who knows what's what in the art world the the name of Dong Kingman is at least as famous for watercolors as the name Guinness is for records. Dong Kingman is that rarity, an artist who is appreciated in his own time. In fact, you might easily say that the California-born artist is one of America's great natural resources.

It is paradoxical that Kingman got into the "Guinness Book of World Records" not for his prowess as an artist, but for feat of signing vast numbers of his popular prints in record time.

When interviewed in his Manhattan studio, the watercolor artist spoke happily of his great preoccupation, his art tours. For years he has been conducting tours for artists to such widely varied places as Venice, the Bahamas, Yosemite National Park and many locations in Mexico. The tours are arranged by Pan Am, the airline with which Kingman has long been associated. Anyone who has ever flown on Pan Am is familiar with Kingman's paintings which he was commissioned to paint for the covers of Pan Am menus. These watercolor illustrations bring a breath of beauty with their fresh, up-beat colors and delicacy of line and perception.

For the past few years Kingman has been conducting artists' seminars in the People's Republic of China.

"As a special-interest group," he stated, "we have received preferential treatment. A tourist in China who isn't a doctor isn't allowed to see the inner workings of a hospital unless he's part of an authorized group of medical men. And a journalist will get to meet newspaper people only if he's in China as a journalist, part of a group of journalists, not just as a tourist. My group being painters, we

Beverly Sills and Dong Kingman in China—both are bringing Western art to China. Miss Sills is helping a new generation of Chinese singers in the art of singing and opera.

were allowed to talk to art people, to visit art academies. Our trip this year—1981—was extra special because of my exhibition over there.

"In 1980 when I was in China with my group I was invited to give a one-man show in China. I came home and spent a year to put the package together. It was a non-profit, cultural exchange thing and I went to almost all the important organizations to solicit money—which is a next to impossible task! You know, everyone has his own worries!

"First I tried the State Department, which said it had no money. Finally I got Pan Am to sponsor the cargo and eventually I got people to support the cause. Finally, I planned the art exhibition for the time my people—my students—would be there. Usually we start our tour in Peking, and the show is held for two weeks each in three Chinese cities—Peking (which they now call Beijing), Hankow (now Hangzhou) and Canton (Guongzhou) so the timing was perfect and the group got a marvelous send-off for their stay in China."

Kingman's tours differ from other tours because ones he conducts are working tours. The artists are there not just to view art, but to paint. Their time is arranged so that they spend at least a half a day painting, and more for those who have already been to China and don't want to spend the rest of the day sightseeing and shopping. However, since many of the artists bring along a non-painting spouse, a full sightseeing program is provided for them, and the two are made to dovetail.

"For instance," says Kingman, "when we go to the Forbidden City in Peking I have the bus take the artists around to the far end, which is most scenic and comfortable for painting, and we paint for several hours while the others are sightseeing all the way through from the front. And at the Great Wall, the artists stay at the base and paint the views while the rest of them climb the Wall as far as they're able. Many of my people are repeat students, and for them it's all paint, paint, paint."

"While you're in China," he was asked, "do you do any painting yourself?"

"Yes, I give demonstrations to the group, and I paint with them, too. I have to be very careful when making plans with Chinese tour guides to see that they allow plenty of time for

Artist Dong Kingman hand-signed 10,000 signatures a day for 12 days for prints of his paintings. At the beginning he signed his name as in the top line above, and gradually, as time went on and he became more and more tired, his autograph became more abstract, and Chinese, as in the lower lines.

painting, so that our time isn't filled with visits to factories and shops as most tours are. It's interesting that the guides, once they got used to the idea, enjoyed simply sitting around and watching us paint instead of running around.

"The tours end with a workshop in Hong Kong. Our seminar lasts five or six days, during which we paint and the students exhibit their paintings for criticism."

"Hong Kong was the scene of the autographing caper that got you a record in the 'Guinness Book of World Records,' wasn't it?" asked the interviewer. "When you say it fast, 120,000 signatures sounds fairly simple. But if you really try to envision the mechanics of signing 120,000 prints at the rate of 10,000 a day, the mind boggles!"

"Well, it was grueling," he said, and the details as he unfolded them sounded very much like the logistics required for a general's plans for a major battle than to set an autographing record.

"To begin with, I know Hong Kong very well. I lived there fourteen years when I was a youngster. The factory where I had to sign was way out in North Point, many miles from downtown Hong Kong. You know, when you have 10 tons of paper involved, you can't move it around! I had to have help to move the paper as I signed it. I phoned the Hong Kong employment people from New York 'You have to supply me with two men at least as helpers,' and they answered, 'No, that's impossible because labor in Hong Kong is very hard to get, especially for a short-term, special job.'

"So I realized I'd have to hire my own people. Obviously my wife was one, and I have one sister already living in Hong Kong. I also have two sisters living in Sacramento whom I convinced to come with me—at my expense, of course. Plus—" and here he laughed—" low union wages.

"We all arrived in Hong Kong in May and I found the hotel which was closest to the factory, to eliminate as much traveling as possible. Everything took planning. To begin with, in order to avoid the heavy Hong Kong traffic we started out each morning at 4 A.M. My sister who lives in Hong Kong called for us with her car and the whole group drove to the factory together. We had to arrange for the night watchmen to be alerted to open the factory for us, for otherwise it was locked up tight at that hour. We started with a cup of coffee and we had a few coffee breaks during the morning, and then we stopped for lunch at 10 o'clock. You know, at 11 all the factory workers go ahead of time to get fast service and a clean place to eat! We ate a quick lunch, and then went back and worked till about 3 or so in the afternoon before we quit for the day.

"My sister, Lily from Sacramento, is the one who really worked out everything. Otherwise in no way could I have accomplished the feat. She used to work in the Seventh Avenue garment business, and has manufactured clothes in Hong Kong for an American firm, so she was familiar with arranging programs. She worked out the routine for handling the paper—the prints of my watercolors that I was to sign. She stationed our work force so that they didn't run into each other. Two other people passed the paper—one brought it to me, and one fanned it out in small batches at a time, lining the papers up so that I could go straight down as I signed. The whole table was covered with lined-up batches and I went from one batch to

Dong Kingman in process of signing 120,000 lithographs in 12 days, surrounded by his helpers—his wife and sisters.

the next. Then another person took it away as I finished and a fourth person restacked it in one of the piles that surrounded us.

"It sounds simple, but the work itself was grueling. Lily fainted a few times, she worked so hard, and my back almost gave out from leaning over to sign.

"As for my signatures, I started out signing my full name, but that took too long—over 3 seconds each. Then I abbreviated it a little and that went faster. Lily kept track of the time and worked out how fast I had to go in order to sign 10,000 times in 10 hours. We also had to allow a little

time off to rest my back by lying down."

"How about your writing hand and fingers?" he was asked.

"That didn't bother me. I hold the pen lightly, as if it were a paintbrush. It was my back that gave out from time to time. But one thing was on our side." He laughed a bit. "Since we had come over from America we found it very easy to get up at 3 o'clock or so in the morning. No jet lag! And when we were finally finished at the end of 10 days, we were all so happy, we celebrated with a champagne party in a Hong Kong restaurant." ■

DOES THE WORLD REALLY LOVE A CLOWN? ASK THE MULTI-TALENTED WILLIE WOPPER

Having fun at the Romper Room TV show is Willie Wopper the Clown during a birthday party for the show.

At 35, after training for months, Willie Hollingsworth made it into the "Guinness Book of World Records" for walking the greatest distance non-stop while balancing a full pint bottle of milk on his head, setting a record of 18½ miles.

This was not his usual occupation. Willie wanted to get into the Guinness Book—but how? Being the world's best clown would require convincing the editors into making a so-called "quality judgement" and the book has only quantitative records. So Willie practiced and practiced until he could walk in perfect balance. Then in 1979

with milk bottle firmly on his head, he walked from his home in Freeport, Long Island, to the Guinness office on Park Avenue in New York.

"Here I am," he said. "I made it."

Willie is known at Shea Stadium where he dances and juggles and performs on top of the dugout about 15 times a year in his white gorilla suit. Just recently he signed a two-year contract as the mascot of the soccer team called the New York United.

"Willie Wopper" Hollingsworth likes playing the "white face" black clown at children's parties best. He has been making children laugh at his

antics for years, and perhaps it's easy for him because that's the way he amuses his five children too. Coming from a poor family failed to dampen his fun. Trained as a concrete finisher, Willie had an number of frustrating experiences after high school but this too has failed to stop him from laughing—especially at himself.

Willie is a self-made clown, a juggler and magician, a multi-talented buffoon, a well-balanced man, with dreams of gaining national fame through the Guinness Book.

When asked "What would inspire a man to do such things?" Willie answered: "It beats working 9 to 5." ■

OMSI
It Stands for Making Science Exciting and Personal

By Diana Kerman
Photos by Phillip Kerman

It would be impossible to select *the most* unusual museum for the "Guinness Book of World Records," but if it could be done, a museum which would certainly be in the running would be the Oregon Museum of Science and Industry—OMSI—located just a few minutes from downtown Portland, Oregon.

From the moment you enter the lobby, all your senses are stimulated. The tiny steel balls of the Gravitram jingle and jangle as they wind their way along a maze of tracks in this electronic kinetic sculpture. Which path will the balls take? Which bell will they ring? Which carriage they will hop upon? It is all difficult to predict. This unusual "Rube-Goldberg"-like sculpture demonstrates various principles of electronics and mechanics.

Next you become a trickle of blood and walk through the atria of an artificial heart that is 14 feet high and 22 feet long. When you've finished examining this coronary giant you can check your own blood pressure and heart beat. An electronic device monitors your heart beat and displays it across a screen that resembles a small TV.

OMSI offers an opportunity to learn more about yourself. The talking transparent lady tells the story of the human body. As she describes each organ, a replica lights up to emphasize its location and function. Exhibits demonstrating the workings of the eyes and ears and the birth process are also featured. A sound-proof booth invites you to "come in and listen." There you will experience sound as it is heard by people with different kinds of hearing defects.

Rube Goldberg used to design contraptions that could have worked. Well this one does work. Tiny steel balls released from above wind their way down to the bottom—and the surprising thing is that without human interference each ball takes its own path, as if it had a mind of its own.

Start here and walk through a pulsating heart. This coronary giant is 14 feet high and 22 feet long.

Want to appeal to your sense of touch? You can cuddle a soft baby chick, after watching it hatch in the incubator. Or you may want to feel the skin of a boa constrictor. OMSI also features a fascinating flat plastic honeycomb where you can view busy bees storing their honey. The bees fly away and return to the hive to do their chores. The queen is always right in the center of activity. While the bees may want to appeal to your sense of touch, this whole exhibit is carefully enclosed in plastic so the bees have plenty of space and you can view it without danger.

No science museum would be complete without a planetarium and OMSI is no exception. Visit the far-off stars and galaxies, listen and watch a cosmic concert or view an unusual light show. At Christmas-

time you can view "the Star of Bethlehem."

And that's just a short view of OMSI.

This unusual museum hosts an unusual auction each year, a highlight of the Portland social scene. You may win a dinner with the Governor, or get a free hysterectomy for your cat, or a free autopsy performed on a loved one by the state medical examiner. The funds raised from the auction, along with grants, and admission and membership fees, are used to defray the cost of the museum.

When you visit the Pacific Northwest and walk through the turnstile of the Oregon Museum of Science and Industry, you will understand a little better the science records in the "Guinness Book." ∎

Inside this plastic honeycomb, thousands of bees are storing their honey, with the queen bee in the center. A whole bee culture is operating, right in front of your eyes.

HIS BED IS HIS OFFICE

World's Most Extraordinary Man Writes Books, Grows Walking Catfish, Takes Photos, Yet Is Paralyzed from Neck Down

by Michele Voso

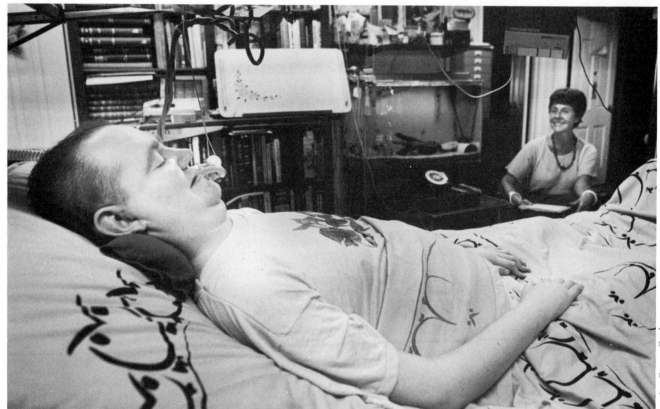

credit: Evans Caglege

Braz Walker talks to Guinness reporter Gail Peterzell from his "office" in Waco, Texas.

Many strange fish records appear in the Animal Kingdom chapter of the "Guinness Book of World Records." Perhaps the most intriguing is a picture of a walking catfish.

When the editors of Guinness received this picture from a man named Braz Walker in Waco, Texas, he pointed out that not only can some species of catfish walk, but others carry an electrical charge of 350 volts at one amp. The walking catfish of Thailand waddles on very strong front fins while pushing itself from behind "snake style," that is, by swishing its tail from side to side. it leaves the water at night and goes on land to hunt or migrate.

When the accompanying letter from Braz Walker was not signed, we merely thought that he had forgotten to sign it. But when a second letter came in unsigned we thought that this was strange. Determined to find out more about this man we finished our work in Houston, and headed for Mr. Walker's home.

Braz, we knew, was an expert on marine life and has had many books and articles published about his discoveries through the research he conducts in his laboratory. He does all his own photography to illustrate his books and the catfish photo he sent us was one he took himself.

The remarkable thing about Braz, 48 years old, is that he has been paralyzed by polio from the neck down since he was 17 years old. He works from his bed surrounded by marvelous mechanical devices that aid him in his research and other endeavors.

Braz's typewriter was developed by an engineer to be used specifically by people with limited movement. It consists of an ordinary IBM electric typewriter, placed beside his bed and wired to a plaque that has figures and letters around the edge in a semi-circle. This plaque is held up by metal arms attached to the headboard and can be lowered and raised in front of Braz when he wants to type. A stylus projects from the plaque. Braz grips the end of the stylus between his teeth and can then manipulate it with his tongue. There are depressions in front of each letter. When the tip of the stylus touches a depression it triggers that letter on the typewriter and the key then strikes the paper.

The paper is inserted and removed by one of the two people who help him 24 hours a day. They also help him with his photography projects.

The camera that Braz uses is set up on a device similar to the typewriter plaque. Braz looks through the lens and tells his helper which f-stop and shutter speed he needs. They set the camera according to his directions, fix the room lighting and then Braz releases the shutter, using his tongue to depress a lever attached to a cable which is screwed into the shutter.

His bed is his office and his communication center. With a telephone device made by IBM and GE specially for him, he talks to reporters, fish buffs and other scientists from around the nation and the world. He can activate the phone too with his tongue, talking into speakers that are placed near his head. An amplification box makes it easy for him to hear the caller. With a CB radio, also operated with his tongue, he talks to his friends and neighbors in and around Waco.

People are always coming and going into and out of Braz's office. TV crews (he was on the "PM Magazine" show), reporters like Gail and me, and legions of school children from the Waco schools.

The children come to hear him tell stories about the fishes in the tanks that line the walls of his office. He also shows them how he works his special typewriter, telephone, CB and camera.

When Braz is not entertaining visitors, writing or editing books, photographing fish or writing his newspaper column, he is very busy finishing up his book of children's stories. These stories are, like the tales he tells to visiting schoolchildren a mixture of fact and fiction calculated to enthrall and educate the reader. ∎

Braz Walker's own walking catfish.

THE WORLD'S MOST SUCCESSFUL COMPLAINER

"Complain Before You're Shafted" Is Ralph Charell's Best Advice

by Gail Peterzell

Do you feel you get "taken" too often? Do you feel your self-esteem is squelched daily by surly clerks and indifferent workmen? Are you a victim of daily social muggings? If your answer to these questions is "yes" you need to know how Ralph Charell is effective in complaining and ultimate winning.

Ralph is in the "Guinness Book" as the Most Successful Complainer. Now, you might envision such a person as a dour curmudgeon who grunts his answers, so this reporter set out to discover just what kind of person a champion complainer might be.

To my amazement Ralph turned out to be an attractive, affable man in his late forties. Ralph is charming, highly articulate, and one of the most reasonable people around.

He says his methods can be used by anyone. "Effective complaining is intended as a means of self-defense, not as another kind of attack, and never as a rip-off. One should defend with honor, but never so vigorously as to become the aggressor."

Charell says "The examples that follow might lead one to assume that I have spent disproportionate time and effort in these pursuits. Perhaps I have in some instances, if success is measured by money alone. But the time I use is always 'down time' and represents, in the aggregate, much less than many people spend on hobbies. The adversaries I challenged always had far greater resources than I. Usually they were large corporations which were clearly, often admittedly, in the wrong, yet resistant to the usual appeals. Although there may have been times when I received more than I deserved (not including the value of my time), that was never my original intention, and it occurred only after the other side had steadfastly refused a lesser settlement. Rationalization? Maybe. But I think I've been fairly reasonable, and I know I feel a lot better now that I've learned from my own

experience that the 'givens' in everyday transactions, are not immutable. They can be challenged—and changed."

Example 1—A Washing Machine

After giving us months of excellent service, our washing machine began to leak. The problem seemed to be caused by a leaky piece of rubber tubing or a faulty connection. My wife called Korvettes, where we'd bought the machine, and learned that its warranty had expired. She was advised to call the Franchised Service Corporation, which would come and repair it at a

After breaking a first appointment, two men from Franchised arrived at our home and announced themselves as "Air conditioning!" They thought they had been sent to remove an air conditioner from our apartment (as Franchised also repairs air conditioners), and they had brought the tools with them to do so.

My wife pointed out that it was a washing machine, not an air conditioner, which needed repair, and asked whether they had brought a replacement for the piece of rubber tubing she had minutely described over the telephone. They had not. They removed the faulty piece of tubing from the machine, demanded and received $10.50 plus tax for the "house call," and promised to return and actually repair the machine in the not-too-distant future.

That night, when my wife summarized the above events for me, it seemed clear that we were being charged for one house call too many. The next morning, I called the man in charge at Franchised. I explained that if his men had known what they were doing, they would have brought the ten-cent piece of rubber tubing in the first place; therefore we should pay only the additional cost of tubing and not for the second house call. Otherwise, I told him, Franchised could return our money and we would go elsewhere.

The Franchised man, in turn, offered me a choice: either I would pay for two house calls plus the price of the part, or they would keep our money and we could go elsewhere.

"Very well," said I. "I will call the store which recommended you and, hopefully, you will be hearing from them soon."

I was shuttled and shuffled from employee to employee, endlessly telling and retelling my dreary tale while my days turned to nights, my mind to jelly. Those who might have helped were busy or vacationing or in meetings. Those I was able to reach didn't understand or lacked jurisdiction. It seemed to me that the Vice President in Charge of Customer Relations was the man who could set things right, but he was never in when I phoned and never returned any of my calls.

A little research revealed that Korvettes is part of a conglomerate owned by Spartans Industries, whose chief executive officer was named Charles Bassine. Many businesses are parts of larger companies, and I have often found it easier to deal with the parent. I usually ask the executive office switchboard operator of the company that is being difficult if there is a parent company. One call to the parent will almost always yield the name of the company president—after all, this is public information. If the name is not immediately forthcoming, it is available at any local brokerage office in Moody's or in Standard and Poor's corporate records, or in most public libraries.

Armed with the chief executive's name, I again called the Vice President in Charge of Customer Relations and was told that he was not at his desk, which came as no surprise.

"In that case," I told his secretary, "perhaps you could give him a message."

"Is it short? I don't take dictation."

"It's not long, and I think Mr.

Ralph Charell is complaining to Guinness Editor David Boehm that some of his records have been left out of the book.

Green* will consider it rather important, so I'll speak slowly while you copy it down."

"What is it?"

"My name is Jennings," said I. "I represent the Charells..."

I explained that the Charells were having some difficulty with Franchised and gave her the address and the model number of the faulty washing machine, as well as the name of the man Charell had spoken with at Franchised and his telephone number.

"The Charells have called the store many times, including a number of calls to Mr. Green, to no avail. As I was only recently remarking to my old friend and classmate, Charlie (the chief executive officer) 'Isn't it a shame that people like the Charells have to call upon me to handle a matter like this when there undoubtedly must be somebody at the store who has the responsibility.' Charlie informed me that Mr. Green was the man to contact. I would suggest that he get a brand-new machine over to the Charells right away so that Charlie won't have to get into this matter personally."

"He just came in, Mr. Jennings. Would you like to speak with him?"

"That won't be necessary. Just give him the message, please. Also, tell him I assume he can have the Charell's money returned from Franchised, as they have done nothing to earn it."

"I'm sure he can, Mr. Jennings. May he get back to you later in the day?"

"As a matter of fact, I'm on my way to the airport right now. I'll be down in Houston on another matter for a couple of weeks but I'll be calling my client in a couple of days to find out what Mr. Green has done."

The next morning, before I left for the office, two men delivered a brand-new machine inside a sealed container, and took away the defective machine. About a week later, an envelope arrived from Franchised containing the piece of rubber tubing they'd taken and their check, reimbursing us in full for the "house call."

*All names in this story which are those of colors are fictitious. All the other names of people and companies are actual.

Example 2—Underwear

On my way to an indoor pool, I picked up a set of underwear at Saks Fifth Avenue. Although I did not have my charge card with me, I showed the salesperson sufficient identification and signed for the eight dollar and three cent purchase. About a month later I received a bill for this

amount and a notice advising me that although I did not have a charge account at Saks, the store would be happy to open one for me if I filled out the enclosed form.

What surprised me most was that the notice set forth both my name and address correctly. That being the case, I was somewhat at a loss as to why the store had failed to locate my account when I had been doing business with Saks for more than twenty years. I returned all of the material received with a handwritten note to this effect and asked them to kindly bill my account.

The following month I received another bill and another notice telling me that I could open an account with the store by filling out the enclosed forms, but would I kindly remit payment in the meantime. Again, I returned all of the material with a handwritten note explaining the situation, across the top of which I wrote in large capitals: "FINAL NOTICE!" If they had sent a computer card I would have punched out some or all of the holes and thus gotten individual treatment.

When I received the same notice a month later, I called the store. The store manager was unavailable, but I was able to speak with one of his assistants.

I told this man that the store had had three opportunities to properly bill my account for the underwear and that if they had done so any one of these times this telephone call and one or both of the handwritten notes would not have been necessary. I explained that as I usually bill between a hundred and a hundred and fifty dollars an hour for my time, it seemed clear that there was no way I could break even on this transaction and that I had dealt with the store for a generation without too much difficulty. The man agreed with me and promised that I would not hear of the matter again.

Charell's solutions result from much time spent in developing new methods of coping with myriad affronts, intransigent rudenesses, deceits, incompetencies, obfuscations, procrastinations, and other unwelcome business practices.

Don't be a loser. You are now aware of some of Charell's techniques. Become courageous, and turn your complaints into dollars, before you get shafted and frustrated. Who knows? You might even beat his Guinness record! ■

HOW THE GUINNESS BOOK BEGAN

The Incredible McWhirter Twins

T hough their inventor grandfather lived in Scotland, Norris and Ross McWhirter were born in London on August 12, 1925, with Norris the older identical twin by twenty minutes. William Mc-Whirter, their father, was the first newspaper editor to edit three national newspapers at the same time, and "subscribed to hundreds of newspapers and magazines," so the Twins always had plenty of reading matter in their home. The senior McWhirter, who had learned and used shorthand, may have been the most compulsive swallower of information of his time. Ross once said that his father simply needed to "know the opposition"—and it is to such eccentricities that the authors of the "Guinness Book of World Records" trace the origin of their interest in fact-gathering.

From an early age the Twins enthusiastically clipped unusual information from the newspapers. "We kept lists of the largest buildings, that sort of thing," Ross told the *Harvard Crimson* in 1975. It was an obsession the brothers never lost. At school they memorized important dates in world history, every river and mountain range, every nation's capital. Later they committed to memory every record in the Guinness Book.

In childhood, the Twins developed their own private language, which they later abandoned for English. Throughout they acted like one person. All that one twin needed to say was something like "Stonehenge is like the Alamo, it's not very impressive" and it would begin a colloquy in which the brothers would correct, and interrupt each other, finish each other's sentences, and leap from one millennium to the next— all of it calmly, perfectly reasonably and in clipped accents as though nothing else could possibly be expected.

"Not very impressive?" "Well, how could it be? Built 1900 years before Christ." "The Pyramids, of course— when were they? A thousand years earlier, I should say..." That's the way the conversation would run whether they were at home, in the office, or on the radio or TV.

The McWhirters in dress garb: Norris is on the left and Ross on the right.

World War II began while the McWhirters were still in school at Marlborough, but in 1943 before they were 18, they were accepted for a 6-month course at Oxford's Trinity College to prepare them for service in the Royal Navy. Ross studied law and Norris history (later economics), as well as signaling, seamanship and naval strategy. Because the British had adopted the so-called Sullivan rule (after five Sullivan brothers had gone down on the same vessel at Guadalcanal) the McWhirter Twins were assigned to different ships, Ross to a minesweeper and Norris to an anti-submarine frigate. It was the first time in their life that they were parted. They served all over the world. Then in 1946, when the war was all but over, in Valetta Harbor, Malta, one fine morning Lieut. Ross McWhirter woke with a bang as the minesweeper he was on was clouted by another ship. Ross rushed up on deck to find that his ship, which was undergoing repairs, had been hit by another British naval vessel, which had had its reversing gear stripped. And who was directing the offending ship but Lieut. Norris McWhirter! Obviously, the Twins were inseparable—even war could not keep them apart.

Released from the Navy, the Twins went back to Oxford. Norris discovered on reading the 300-page book of university regulations that an ex-serviceman was allowed to take exams and qualify for a degree in three terms rather than the usual nine—namely 1 year as compared to 3. So Norris obtained his degree in economics in three terms, and Ross his degree in law (a more demanding subject) in five terms.

Norris now took "a brief spell in accounting" with a London firm while waiting for Ross to "come down" from Oxford. In 1949 they started in the fact-finding business, a unique enterprise at the time. The company called McWhirter Twins, Ltd. did research mainly for encyclopedias, periodicals, yearbooks and advertisers.

Through being enterprising, Norris picked up a news story about the official hangman and sold it to the *Star* newspaper, and this led to the Twins being hired as correspondents on tennis and rugby (Ross) and track and field (Norris), a relationship that lasted for nine years. Their first story about records (which they called "superlatives") was accepted by a boy's magazine called *Eagle*. In that first year, Norris started as a commentator for the BBC, assisting on sports.

Besides running in track events, the Twins in 1951 were hired to work on the sports section of the *News of the World Almanac* and they also started publishing a monthly magazine called *Athletics World.* By the end of 1952, the magazine had subscribers in 54 countries, many of them statisticians themselves.

In 1954, the main achievement was Roger Bannister's breaking the 4-minute mile, while Norris did the commentary for spectators and radio. Bannister had been Norris' and Ross' teammate for Britain at Oxford and elsewhere, and this true "milestone" event got worldwide attention.

On the same track team was a runner named Chris Chataway, later holder of the world record at 5,000 meters, who had been at Oxford with the McWhirters and who was now working for the Guinness brewery. The Guinness managing director at the time was Sir Hugh Beaver, whose hobby was shooting. One day when he was out in the field with friends he took a shot at a bird, a golden plover, and missed. Since he prided himself on his aim, Sir Hugh turned to his companions and said, "I wonder how fast that bird was flying?" Reference to various encyclopedia failed to reveal the information as to how fast the golden plover could fly or what the record speed was for any bird. Sir Hugh felt that such big expensive reference books should include such records, and some time later got the idea that "records were just the things that started pub and bar arguments all over the world and it was about time somebody produced a book full of records that could settle this kind of dispute."

Chris Chataway was asked if he knew of anyone who could turn this idea into reality, and he said he knew some twins "just down from Oxford" who already had a fact-and-figure agency and who could quote records of all kinds at will. Chris rang up the Twins and asked them to come to the brewery just outside London for a confidential lunch with Sir Hugh without Chris.

Norris tells the story in his own words best in the book he wrote in 1975 called "Ross": "On 12 September 1954 Ross and I drove together to Park Royal, an impressive 54-acre layout which even had level crossings and traffic lights within the complex dominated by three massive brick-built buildings. We were met by the director's messenger and taken along to the board dining room where there was a considerable turn-out of directors but no other guests. Sir Hugh seemed to be gently but firmly

Father had been a champion fly-weight boxer and the Twins, Norris (left) and Ross (right), received boxing gloves on their seventh birthday.

in command....After the usual general conversation Sir Hugh led it round to the subject of records and record-breaking. Ross and I were asked the records for a number of what to us were fairly simple categories, such as filibustering (Senator Wayne Morse of Oregon, over 22 hours) and pole-squatting (a man in Portland also in Oregon called Howard who stayed up for 196 days). Lord Moyne (one of the several peers on the Guinness board, sometimes internally referred to as "the beerage") was more interested in how one found out, rather than if we knew the answer, and posed the question how, for instance, would one discover the identity of the widest river that had ever frozen.

"Ross replied, before I could, that this particular problem was really quite simple because it could lie between three contenders namely the three main Russian rivers, the Ob, the Yenisey and the Lena which flowed into the Arctic, adding that the Antarctic did not of course have any rivers.

"Sir Hugh then began talking about his experiences in Turkey, and mentioned the problems of translating from English into Turkish...I interposed that I could not see why since Turkish had only one irregular

verb. Sir Hugh stopped dead and said 'Which is the irregular verb?' I replied 'imek, to be.' 'Do you speak Turkish?' he asked, so I admitted I didn't. 'Then how on earth do you know that?' he queried. 'Because records of all kinds interest me and I had learnt that fact in trying to discover which language had fewest irregular verbs compared with the 180 or so in English.'

"Sir Hugh seemed to decide that he had discovered people with the right kind of quirkish mind for producing the book, which he now resolved should be published under the Guinness imprint, to settle arguments in the 81,400 pubs in the country. Quite suddenly he said: 'We are going to set up a publishing subsidary. Which one of you is to be Managing Director?' Ross explained that he had a job in Fleet Street and I would be better placed to take on the assignment. Sir Hugh who was by now anxious to get off to another appointment, merely added: 'Before you leave go up and see the acountant and tell him how much money you need'."

As they drove back to London Norris and Ross realized that they had almost casually been talked into agreeing to take on a monumental task, gathering together information that had never appeared in print before, but this was something they could do and wanted to do. As Norris said, "It was going to be a very tough and challenging task. However we were still in our twenties... We may as well do the thing properly and vigorously under the auspices of a great and clearly most civilized company. Yes, we could and would do it and do it flat out."

Target date for the book was July 1955. The Twins hired an office manager and the three of them worked until late into the small hours night after night.

Work on the book consisted of extracting "ests" (highest, lowest, smallest, oldest, fastest, heaviest, etc.) from "ists" (ichthyologists, paleontologists, dendrochronologists, etc.) The Twins soon learned how to go about it. When writing to an expert they did not ask for a direct bit of information, but stated a fact that they figured might be close to being right and asked the expert to correct it. "We found that people who have a total resistance to giving information," Norris wrote, "often have an irresistible desire to correct other people's impressions."

In June and July 1955 the stream of letters which they had sent out to experts all over the world had begun to yield a full harvest. The Twins had to arrange for the printing and binding of the book as well. By August 27, 1955, less than a year after getting their assignment, the Twins received in their hands the first copy of the "Guinness Book of Records." Hard-bound, with more than 200 pages, full of illustrations, it sold for the unheard-of price of 5 shillings (about 75¢). It was not an instant success despite the low price. Some 50,000 copies had been printed and the first call was made on W.H. Smith, the largest book supplier in Britain. The disappointing order was for 6 copies. Smith's was known for its conservatism, but this was a bit much. As the sales manager called on the retail stores, orders flowed into Smith's, so within a short time their initial order was increased from 6 to 100, then to 1,000, and by the end of one week to 10,000.

This first edition contained British records as well as world records, and the McWhirters were pleased with their "baby" except for one oversight—the record for the fastest bird had been omitted! ∎

Athletically inclinded, the McWhirter Twins were on Oxford's track team with Roger Bannister. Here Norris (left) takes over the baton in a victorious relay race.

How Guinness Came to America

by David A. Boehm
American Publisher and Editor

It was before 8 in the morning on a sunny winter day in 1957 in Boston when I arrived at the DeWolfe and Fiske bookstore on Park Street, opposite the Common in Boston. Morton DeWolfe, owner and buyer, always came in early and liked seeing book salesmen (travelers, we were called) without any interruption before customers arrived. To my dismay, the door was still locked, and ahead of me was a Doubleday salesman with 50 new titles in his bag ready to be discussed and sold that month—at least 2 hours was a fair estimate of how long it would take.

What to do? Call on other shops? No one else was open except the New England News Co. and their warehouse was at the edge of town. No, wait my turn was the logical thing to do.

When Morton arrived, he sized up the situation, If perhaps I had only one or two titles to sell, the Double-day salesman might well have let me go ahead of him. But I had Sterling's biggest Spring list—15 titles—so I wisely said to Morton "I'll browse around the stacks, and see you as soon as you can see me." Morton acquiesced and was pleased.

The DeWolfe store was big and old-fashioned and the stacks were high. Thousands of books met my eye. One, I noticed, had a white jacket among all the reds and blues and blacks. Remember, it was 1957 and white jackets were frowned upon to some extent by booksellers because they got marred and scarred easily. This one had a strange title. In big print was the word SUPERLATIVES with some small type on the left and below. In the upper right-hand corner was a cartoon of a fat man 7'8" high who apparently weighed 1000 lbs., holding in his hand another man only 20½" high. Intriguing. The other illustrations were little square color blocks with a

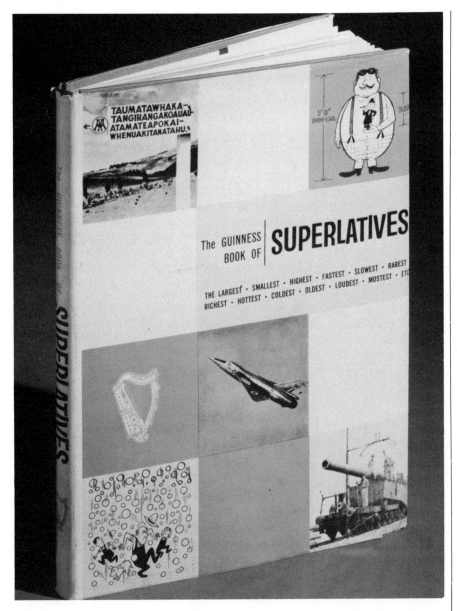

RUPERT GUINNESS

September 1956·   Earl of Iveagh

If you needed a reason to publish a record book, this was a good one. And who *was* the tallest president? I looked in the back for an index and found a complete one. Of course, it was Lincoln at 6 feet 4½ inches. Who was the author? No name on the title page. Strange. But there was a Preface signed by THE COMPILERS—no names.

PREFACE

This book is a collection of facts—finite facts expressed in quantitative terms, predominantly those which by measurement are superlative or are records in their respective fields. The world's greatest man is, for this book, the man with the greatest girth rather than the man with the greatest intellect.

Many of the data contained within these pages are by their very nature constantly changing. In 1953 the Nebula Andromeda, the most distant heavenly body visible to the naked eye, was discovered to be twice as far away as had hitherto been thought. In February 1955, the Russians announced the discovery of a new mountain in Siberia higher than any in America, Europe or Africa. No reference book such as this can ever claim to have said the last word.

It would be impracticable to mention all the vast number of sources and references which attach to each of the items included in this volume. In the event of rival claims for a particular superlative, it has been the sole responsibility of the compilers to weigh up the evidence and to come to a decision.

We wish to acknowledge the generous assistance of countless experts from all over the world who have aided us, and we shall greatly welcome comments and suggestions from our readers who have reason for criticizing our researchers or can add to our information. In that way, we can hope to improve and enlarge any future editions.

THE COMPILERS.
SUPERLATIVES INC.
270 Madison Avenue
New York 16
MUrray Hill 3-7634/5

By this time I was convinced that the publishing of this volume was a worthwhile enterprise. I kept on reading. One item read:

2. Longevity

Medical men, who have devoted themselves to the study of old age (gerontolo-

---

signpost on one, an uptilted airplane on another, a harp on a third, a big cannon on another, and finally a cartoon, of farmers dodging hailstones. Quite a melange! But what exactly are superlatives and what kind of a book can be written about them? In insignificant type was the name GUINNESS, which I hadn't noticed before. Of course, I knew Alec Guinness and Guinness Stout, but where did they come in?

Morton had 3 copies of this title on the shelf. I picked up one, opened it to a page that said *Oklahoma* was the world's most successful musical comedy and Walt Disney had won the most Oscars—24. There most be dozens of books about records like this, I thought. Another page revealed that fact that the only U.S. president who was a bachelor was James Buchanan. Who cares? I

thought. The page also said that William Henry Harrison (I knew he was president for only 30 days) had 14 children. I didn't know that! And Andrew Johnson had a 17-year-old wife! Where did all these odd facts come from? I wondered.

Naturally, as I was a publisher, I looked next at the copyright page. It was in the name of Superlatives, Inc. and was printed in New York.

The Foreword was a noble effort concerned with helping settle arguments.

FOREWORD

Wherever people congregate to talk, they will argue, and sometimes the joy lies in the arguing and would be lost if there were any definite answer. But more often the argument takes place on a dispute of fact, and it can be very exasperating if there is no immediate means of settling the discussion.

gists), do not give credence to reports of people living much beyond 110 years. Few subjects have been so obscured by deceit and falsehood. The most extreme claims are for a man of 185 years (variously 187) named Setrasch Czarten (also Petratsh Zarten) allegedly born near Teneswaer, in Hungary, in 1537, and alive in 1722 and for a woman of 175 years named Louisa Trousco, a South American negress, who died circa 1776.

The authenticity of the age of Christian Jacobsen Drakenberg (died October 19th, 1772) who reputedly lived to an age of 145 years 325 days is widely believed in Scandinavia. The evidence that it was he who was born in Denmark on November 8th, 1626, is unacceptable since there is a discontinuity of 15 years in the chronicle of this allegedly single life. A considerable amount of ex post documentation exists upon the age of the illiterate Spanish serving woman, Maria Josefa Nieto Santos, who died in Madrid on December 21st, 1906, at a reputed 125 years and 75 days. A certified baptismal certificate pointing to a birth date on October 7th, 1781, was produced after her death.

I kept on reading. Here were the heaviest man and the smallest dwarf on page 10. Here was the mother of 69 children, a woman who had "tresses" 8 feet 3 inches long, a man who jumped on ice over 15 barrels, a French tightrope walker who made it across Niagara Falls with a man on his back, a lion tamer of 40 beasts, and more and more. I couldn't put the book down.

There were pictures among the 224 pages, and records from all over the world, but most of the records were American.

So absorbed did I become that I didn't notice that the Doubleday salesman had left. Morton came out and I told him to skip me and take the next traveler as I had found a book to read. He looked at me quizically, but went ahead.

At about 11 o'clock I had seen enough of "Superlatives" to know that this was a book that would sell even if there were other books of records, because "the compilers," whoever they were, had selected interesting items from the many basic statistics and treated them with humor.

When I finally sat down with Morton, I had the "Superlatives" book in my hand. "Are there many other record books like this?" I asked him.

"The World Almanac and other almanacs are all I know of," was his reply.

"Well, when did you get this?" was my next question.

"Not long ago," was his reply, "and I didn't get it from a salesman. I must have seen an ad for it and ordered it from that address on the title page. We ordered 10 and now we're down to 3, but they haven't filled my reorder."

I promised to follow up with the company at 270 Madison Avenue in New York, the address on the title page.

When I did return to my office in New York, I remembered that my salesman in the West, Charlie Johnson, had asked me to get more books and publishing lines for him to carry, as he was not making enough money. (Neither was I nor my company.) I wrote Charlie and told him to pick up a copy of "Superlatives" and see what he thought of it as an item to add to his briefcase. Charlie's reply was typical of his vision: "I think the book is really great and I'd like to sell it. Why don't you take it on for a complete Sterling distribution?"

His enthusiasm impelled me to approach it differently. I called the Superlatives, Inc. office and a Dorothy Nelson answered me. When I asked if she needed any help in distributing the book, she said "Oh, I would be grateful if you would come and talk to me about it."

Before I did that, I checked in "Books in Print" for other books of records and was amazed when I couldn't find any but the almanacs.

Miss Nelson was a young-looking elderly lady all alone in a very small room loaded with copies of *the* book, loose, and in cartons. She confessed to me that she couldn't keep up with both the shipping of orders and the checking-in of returns. Her only help was a schoolboy who came in at 3:30. Also she was having great trouble collecting from the bookstores. I gave her some sound advice, like not shipping to questionable accounts.

"What's questionable?" she asked. "I have no way of checking credit."

I also told her to send out statements to stores that were delinquent.

"When will I get time for that? Oh, I wish somebody would take over this distribution. The Brewery (in Long Island City) can't give me any help."

She showed me a file of clippings of reviews of the book from important publications of the time—all rave reviews. In many cases they quoted records from the book, and

some reviews said there had never been a book like this before. Certainly some specialists and organizations had kept records, but no one had ever put a wide range of records into book form. I was, and still am, amazed that such a natural idea never came into print before.

Miss Nelson said she thought, as an American, that the title "Superlatives" was confusing, and while the book had sold 18,000 copies it was far from the 50,000 that had been optimistically printed by the Guinness company for America. No promotion had been done, no mailing to bookstores, only review copies to newspapers and magazines and a small ad in *Publishers Weekly*.

"From what you tell me, I'd say 18,000 was a good sale even though the price of $2.95 is very low for a big hard-cover book." That was my opinion.

"Would you take over the distribution?"

Would I! I felt certain I could promote it right.

"Well, get in touch right away with Norris McWhirter in England and suggest that." Apparently Norris, managing director of Superlatives, Inc., had just been in the U.S. and I had just missed him. I wrote.

Meanwhile, I took home a copy of the book and left it on my desk. My son, Lincoln, 12 years old, took it to bed with him one night, stayed up late reading it and told me next morning that we should be selling it. That was the last word I needed. The reviews, plus Morton, Charlie, Lincoln—all enthusiastic—and, I was entranced by the book myself on first cracking it open.

When Norris invited me to come see him in England, I accepted readily. We agreed that he would pick me up at the Grosvenor House Hotel in London and take me to dinner. It was my initial trip to Europe, and I was going to the Frankfurt Book Fair first.

When I got to London and checked into the hotel, there was Norris, right on time. (I later learned he had never been on time before—or since!) He immediately whisked me out to his mother's home in the northern suburbs of London where he had arranged a dinner party that included Dr. Arthur Hughes, Norris' brothers, Ross and Kennedy Mc-Whirter, Norris' fiancée Carole and Ross' wife Rosemary. Dr.

Ross (left) and Norris McWhirter looking over first proofs of the "Guinness Book" in their London office.

Hughes was the managing director of the Guinness parent company, the brewery, also chairman of Superlatives, the publishing division. Ross, Norris' twin, was also his partner in preparing the book, and Kennedy, a geneticist they called "the smart one." Norris' mother, with the aid of a French chef, had prepared a magnificent dinner. Nobody said a word about business until after the gentlemen had retired to the drawing room for coffee.

Then Dr. Hughes handled the questioning. Although a larger company than Sterling, and a publisher with more than 8 years experience, would have been more to his liking, our very smallness and enthusiasm for the book were appealing. I pointed out that the Guinness book would be our major title and we would push it more than a big, diversified publishing house

would or could. The upshot was, after an hour of discussion, that my seeking them out made the difference and I convinced the group that Sterling should take over the remaining 32,000 copies in stock in New York, sell them to the trade, and pay for them as we sold them. The price was reasonable and so began our connection with Guinness, and the launching of the book under a new title and under American auspices.

At this time, Sterling had perhaps 150 books in print after a modest start in 1949 with 6 titles. All of our office staff of 5 and our sales staff of 6 **devoted** our attention to the book, now rejacketed with a picture of a loving cup and new title "Guinness Book of World Records." It took us 4 years to sell out the 32,000 copies despite great publicity. The U.S. was just not ready for a records book.

When we sold out in 1960, I visited Norris McWhirter's own home and suggested that we produce in America a paperback edition of the "Guinness Book" with just world records, where the first edition had world *and* American records. We would make it up from proofs of the British edition which was so successful that it was being published yearly. We agreed on the spot to do it that way, we agreed on a royalty, and we signed a piece of paper in Norris' kitchen which became know as the Kitchen Memo. Surprisingly, it was the only written contract we had until 1973, when the Guinness lawyers asked to check a point in "the contract" and found none in the files.

No sooner did the paperback edition come out in 1960 than the bookstores asked to have a hardcover edition. So we took some copies of the paperback and bound them up in hardcovers.

It wasn't until late 1961 that we brought out a new hardcover edition, typeset from stratch in America. We didn't plan to publish annually as the British did—just republish and update each time we ran out of stock, which turned out to be every year and a half. We "went annual" in 1973 finally. (That's why our 19th edition dated 1981 corresponds to the 27th British edition, as you bibliophiles may be interested to know.)

I was in Frankfurt at the Book Fair in 1961 when I got a cable from my wife, who was holding the office together, saying that Bantam Books wanted to buy the paperback rights to "Guinness" for a small sum as an advance against royalty. I was pleased but I cabled back that she should ask 10 times as much. When she got the cable, she thought I had gone out of my mind or else the cable was wrong, so she did nothing. I returned to N.Y. in a week or so and made the deal with Bantam at 5 times their first offer. Bantam published its first paperback edition in 1962 and since then has sold somewhere in the neighborhood of 25 million copies, while Sterling has sold another 6 million. Total sales worldwide including Britain have now passed the 42½ million mark.

The "Guinness Book of World Records" has become the fastest selling book in the world! It has also sold more copies than any other copyrighted book (the Bible is not copyrighted) in the world. ∎

GUINNESS:
Letters to the Editor

Dear Sir or Madame:

My daughter Crystal Lutz is running out of room in our house for her collection of 20,000 beer bottle caps.

I was in touch with the Hamilton Public Library and they said that you need a news report or a newspaper clipping.

As you can see in the picture they were very interested, as she made the front page and, also a write up on page 7.

If you feel that this is a new record, could you please get in touch with me one way or another.

Mrs. Donna Lutz
P.S. We are still going strong on collecting beer caps.

Dear Sir,

I have just broke a record. Everyone was trying to get to the center of a lollipop, that is the tootsie roll lollipop, without biting into it so it took me 250 licks to get to the center of the tootsie lollipop. I was wondering if this was important enough to be put in the Guinness world book of records. this is my name. Mrs. J.A.W. thats my married name. I don't know if this is important but if it is please let me know because I've always wanted to do something really neat. I know that I'm not the best at anything at all. But I guess I will give it the best that I've got. I really can draw lots of things. My brother can also draw cars and also vans and 18 wheelers. I thought that I would give it a try at it. This is the biggest thing that I have ever done in my life. This means alot to me ok. THANKS ALOT!

Please let me know alright!

sincerely yours,
Mrs. J.A.W.

To whom it may concern,

I am 11 years old and I can beat every car going down our street on my bike. My bike is not a 10 speed, just a regular bike. I was wondering if you were interested. Also my cousin's father's dog Lady has been around since the beginning of World War II. She is a very old dog. In the 1978 Guinness Book of World Records it says that Dr. Allen Abbott rode his bike at 140.4 m.p.h. I maybe can't go that fast but I can go fast. If you don't believe me send someone to test me. I'll be ready. Don't think I'm just a silly little kid either.

Sincerely
Gretchen B.

Kaz Novak

Crystal Lutz is running out of room for her collection of beer bottle caps. The 6-year-old Hamilton, Ontario, girl thinks she's entitled to inclusion in the Guinness Book.

My dear subjects,

I am your Queen through a Miracle by God. I work at times as a spy in my job of Ruler, I am chosen Ruler by God for God like Noah was.

I would like for my son Prince Philip Emmanuel who will be 14 years old tomorrow and me to be written up in the Guinness Book. God sees everything you do. My child was kidnapped from me by the U.S. court system, but would be returned to me if I would stop saying am Queen.

I have been locked up more times than anyone I know of in history.

Queen Carol
Chosen Ruler by God
Miami, Florida

Dear Guinness:

Hi! How are you? I hope you are fine!

The reason for this letter is that I wish to set a world's record for bus riding! Buses are my means of transportation & has been for about 6 years now. I enjoy riding tremendously!

The Southern California Rapid Transit District (RTD) is one alternative to the automobile. I always carry a pack of bus schedules with me & are always giving them out to people! Sometimes even the drivers ask me for information or schedules.

Here is a little information about me:

Age: 27½ (look about 18)
Instruments played: accordion, organ, sax.
Personal points: Dark brown hair, brown eyes, 5'6½ 117 lbs.
Have a nice day!

O.G.B.
Los Angeles, Calif.

Dear Editor:

My friend and I are going to try for a world record. We read your book but did not see any records about making a whirlpool in a swimming pool by walking in a circle. Would you please tell us it there is one?

What day should we start? If it is raining out what other day should we do this? My friend Billy is eight years old and I Michelle is twelve years old.

It is ok with our parents.
Please send us any information we might need about rules, etc.

Thank you.
M.P. & B.P.
Hickory Hills, Ill.

Dear Sirs:

My friend and I are nine years old and we would like to know how you go about setting a record for the Guinness? If there is no record already set how is a record started? The record we were curious about was a Woosh Record as to how long someone could keep a Woosh going back and forth. Also if there is a record please let us know. We would appreciate your letting us know, thank you.

Eddy and Brad

Gentlemen:

I wish to inform you of my 18-year-old son's teeth growing in his nose. He has two teeth growing (one full tooth on the right side & a small one on the left side). These are extra teeth. The roots are joined in his mouth & the teeth are inverted in his nose. So far four (4) doctors have looked at him & they have never seen anything like it.

We have the X-rays to prove the above.

If you are interested in learning more about the above please contact me.

I remain
(Mrs) P.M.Z.

Dear Guinness

Have you heard about the man who calls himself "the undisputed hug champion"? He lectures before big audiences, as many as 5,000 at a time, and stays after the lecture to hug anyone and everyone who wants to meet him and be hugged. Nearly half of each audience patiently stands in line to get a hug from Leo.

Can you cofirm that Leo is the undisputed record holder?

Steven Short
Los Angeles

Editor's Note:
If we could establish a definition for a hug such as whether you need to use both arms, how long the hug needs to be held, etc., then we would begin to collect records on this sport, and if we had enough claimants, and they could prove their claims, then we might possibley include the category along with kissing in future editions of the Guinness Book or Guinness Magazine and perhaps Mr. Buscaglia, if he keeps track of the number of his hugs, might become the champion and King of Hugs.

Dear Guinness:

I think your wonderful Guiness Book of World Records would not accept the following facetious account. Can you advise a publication that would? The longest time that a dog has churned in a complete cycle of a washing machine and lived as active as ever is fifteen minutes. (It was a Chihuahua, immediately named Maytag.)

Bob S.
Reno, Nevada

Dear Norris McWhirter,

I think I have found the longest Indian Word. This word is a lake that the Indians lived near.
Lake Chargoggagogmanchauggagogg-chaubunagungamaugg.

I hope it is. If so please let me know.

From,
S.C.

P.S. Please send me any other information that I will need to break any other record. Thank you.

To whom it may concern,

I am one of the million readers of your book. I think it ingenious that you collect unique events and personalities. I myself have something unique I have discovered during my childhood and still going on. Everytime I urge and touch my eyelids with the use of only one finger, ballpen, arm, any solid object with edge and many more. This action imediately results in my eyelid popping out, exposing the inner skin. So far during demonstration to friends none of them can imitate me. They can do it only with the use of two fingers twisting out the inner skin of the eyelid.

I hope you will spend time to examine my letter and to take action.

Yours respectfully,
Chingcuanco, Wilson
Manila, Philippines

Dear Person,

In spring of 1973, I caught in central California a pollywog of a common Tiger Salamander. I've hand-raised her and she reached a length of almost 12 inches and a weight of 170 grams (6 oz.) Is she the largest? I feed her on a delicious diet of raw liver, crickets, mealworms and raw hamburger. How may I get her included in the Guinness Book?

C.R.M.
Agoura, Calif.

Guinness,
2 Park Avenue,
New York, N.Y. 10016
Dear publisher of the Guinness Book of World Records:
I would like to know how to get in touch with Guinness. Please send me the address.
                                                                                C.C.G.
                                                                    Columbus, Ohio

Dear Guinness Editor:

It's just uncanny!!!

This is what 40,000 plus alumimmum cans look like when they are strung into a four-mile length and arranged to spell out the name of the collecting group. Those Hagen Junior High science club members surrounding the cans are hoping to make the Guinness Book of World Records.

The students started collecting the cans shortly before the holidays and showed up at school this week with 100-foot strings. Proceeds from the sale of the cans will go toward a roast pig supper for their parents, some of whom enjoyed providing the empties for the string.

Bill Andrus
Dickinson, N.D.

Dear Sirs:

I am writing to tell you, or rather confirm, the fact that a guinea pig by the name of Sopwith Camel, to the best of my knowledge, holds the fastest time for climbing sixteen stairs (with two landings) in the amazing time of 4½ seconds.

Attached please find a list of the signatures of witnesses who watched this spectacle on the date of Wednesday, September 28, 1977 at 10:30 p.m.

Sincerely yours,
J.H.M.

Dear Guinness:

Please send me information on how to get entered into Guinness records. Do I have to have a picture of the event?

I have made a string of gum wrappers on July 19 it was 659 inches. I have a sample of how it is made, enclosed. My mother helped out by chewing most of the gum.

M. McA.
Niagara Falls, New York

Editor's Note: We don't carry records of ordinary collections, such as this or chains of paper clips, pop tops from aluminum cans, pennies, four leaf clovers, flower chains, pebbles, picture cards, matchbook covers, empty boxes, toothpicks, rubber bands, pencils, nuts or acorns, bottle caps, beer tabs, tin cans, etc., etc.

Dear Guinness:

I believe that I have the longest eyelash in the world. It is about 2" long. Contact me if you feel I have room in your book. Please—before it falls out.

Coquitlam, B.C.
J.M.

Dear Guinness:

At school I was looking at the Guinness Book and I noticed that there wasn't any record for the longest eyebrow. I have an eyebrow that is about 3½" long. I was wondering if you wanted to check this out.

J.B.
Lewisville, Ohio

Editor's Note: Neither of these compare with the eye of the squid which is bigger than a long-playing phonograph record—that is, 15" in diameter. Just think—if the squid had eyelashes and eyebrows! ■

HOW TO GET INTO THE GUINNESS BOOK

Answers to Some Commonly Asked Questions

■ ABOUT CATEGORIES

Q. *What record can I break?*

A. You have the greatest chance of getting your record into the book if you attempt a record that is already in the book. Don't ask the editors to pick a category for you or tell you which records are "easy" to break. The worldwide competition to set records has been so great, even in the most unusual categories, that almost all of the standing records are products of outstanding efforts. Your ability to break a record will depend on your particular skills and determination.

Q. *Is there an entry fee or registration form?*

A. No. It is not necessary to register with Guinness before attempting a world record, although it's a good idea to check the rules and find out the latest record. Guinness does not sponsor or lend its name to record attempts, but merely reports records that have been set and verified. While Guinness is all in favor of your trying to set a world record, you should know that you are *legally prohibited* from using the Guinness name or Guinness book name in any way with your attempt.

Q. *I want to set a record in a category that is not in the book. Will you accept it?*

A. Probably not. The Guinness book is a general reference work that simply cannot accommodate all of the possible record categories in one volume. As such, the editors have selected those records that generate the most interest and competition. Only when an event does become subject to widespread and international competition, is Guinness likely to establish a new category in the book.

Q. *But if it's not in the book then whatever I do will be the record, right?*

A. Wrong, at least 99 times out of 100. Guinness will only publish a record when we feel certain that it is a record. If we have not collected information on a subject, we will reserve judgment until we have completed research. Often, the lack of information reflects a lack of interest, and the category will be rejected. You must realize that Guinness is not interested in giving away "easy" world records, and a performance in a new category must be very impressive before it will be considered.

Q. *I watched a TV show, and they said they had set a world record. I can do better. Will I get into the book?*

A. Records claimed on TV (whether a Guinness-labeled show or any other) are not usually set under conditions that the book editors will accept and so are not necessarily records for the book. Statements made on TV—and in the newspapers —are loosely called world records, and often are not acceptable. Better to use the published book as your guide.

Q. *This really unusual thing happened. Will you put it in the book?*

A. Unique occurrences and interesting peculiarities are not in themselves necessarily records. For Guinness to enter a record, it must be competitive and, therefore, measureable. Contrary to popular opinion, Guinness is not interested in freakish events *per se,* although many records are themselves highly unusual happenings.

Q. *Even though this may not be the overall world record, it's the most done on a Tuesday by left-handers under 10 years of age in a town of less than 2,000 people. Will you include it?*

A. No way. There simply is no room in the Guinness book for records that are limited to special conditions, age groups, or by the addition of endless sub-categories.

Q. *Do you have any kid's records?*

A. The "Guinness Book of World Records" has very few categories specifically for young people. Only a handful of significant achievements, such as successfully swimming the **English Channel,** include records for the youngest (and oldest) performers.

REST BREAKS

Human Achievements (Chapter 11 of the book)

Those events listed are continuous and rest breaks are *not* allowed. (Those marked * are solo records. The others are relays, worked on a shift basis.)

Baby Carriage Pushing
Bed of Nails*
Bed Pushing
Brick Carrying*
Egg and Spoon Racing*
Joke Telling*
Kiss of Life
Leap Frogging
Milk Bottle Balancing*
Pole Sitting'
Stretcher Carrying
Tree Sitting*

Sports, Games and Pastimes (Chapter 12 of the book)

Endurance events in this chapter fall roughly into five categories.

MARATHON: Five-minute breaks allowed for resting, etc., *after* every completed hour of play (optional but aggregable).

VIRTUAL NON-STOP: Minimal breaks permitted for essential medical/toilet purposes, but no breaks whatsoever for resting.

ABSOLUTE NON-STOP: No breaks at all allowed.

CONTINUOUS: Performed on a rotating or relay basis.

SKILL/ENDURANCE: Breaks permitted as and when necessary.

(Those activities marked † are not reported in the "Guinness Book of World Records," but they are eligible to be reported in the "Guinness Book of Sports Records, Winners and Champions.")

MARATHONS

Badminton—singles, doubles
Basketball
Bowling (10-pin)
†Croquet
†Curling
Equestrian
†Backgammon
†Chess
†Cribbage
†Darts
†Dominoes
Pool (billards type)
†Monopoly
†Scrabble
†Field Hockey
†Horseshoe Pitching
Ice Skating
Roller Skating
Skiing—Alpine/Nordic
Soccer—5 and 11 a side
Softball—fast and slow pitch
Squash
Treading Water
Table Tennis—singles, doubles
Tennis—singles, doubles
Trampolining (solo)
Volleyball
Water Polo
Water Skiing

VIRTUAL NON-STOP

Cycling   Running
Swimming   Walking

ABSOLUTE NON-STOP

Stationary Cycling
Rope Jumping (no misses)
Soccer Ball Control—Juggling/Heading
Swimming—longest continuous
Table Tennis Rally

CONTINUOUS

†Roller Cycling—four man (rotating)
†Contract Bridge (rotating)
†Darts—million and one (rotating)
†Tiddlywinks (rotating)
Judo (rotating)
Swimming Relays
Track and Field Relays
Trampolining—team (rotating)

SKILL/ENDURANCE

Archery—24 hours
Basketball—accuracy
Canoeing—eskimo rolls
†Roller Cycling—solo
†Darts—10 hours, 24 hours
Pool—24-hour pocketing
Golf—most rounds (on foot)
Gymnastics (breaks permitted provided position is maintained during break) — chinning, parallel bar dips push-ups. jumping jacks, somersaults.
Parachuting—24 hours
Shooting—24 hours
Skiing—24-hour distance
Swimming—24 hours
Track and Field—24 hours, 100 miles
Walking—24 hours, backwards 24 hours
Weight Lifting—24 hours
†Yachting—24 hours

However, youngsters have set many Guinness records competing with people of all ages, and many of these appear also in the "Guinness Book of Young Record-breakers." You should realize that many of the records are difficult to set, so don't take on something that will be too much for you. Be sure to involve your parents and other adults in the attempt. Also, it is a good idea to check with your doctor so you know how to get ready for what will surely be a strenuous effort.

Q. *This record attempt is being done for charity, so does that make it qualify?*

A. Although Guinness whole heartedly encourages any connection between record attempts and raising money for good causes, all records must nevertheless stand on their own. Hence, a charity's sponsorship will not affect the acceptance of a record. However, charities can often be helpful in organizing your effort and you may find that helping others provides a reservoir of extra strength and determination.

■

ABOUT RULES
Q. *What do I do to break a record?*

A. You should compete *exactly* with the previous record. If, for example, you are challenging the doughnut-eating record, you must consider the total weight, as well as the number, of doughnuts. If you challenge the record for sit-ups, you must perform them without feet pinned or knees bent. If there is a national governing body for an activity, you must consult it for rules and, it is strongly recommended, involve one of its representatives as an official, for no Guinness editor will be present. If there is any doubt about the rules, you should follow the strictest interpretations. If you write or call up Guinness for information, be sure to call long enough in advance of your planned attempt to allow the editors time to collect information and rules interpretations.

Q. *What are the rules for rest breaks?*

A. Not all activities permit rest breaks. See the chart here for a description of the various kinds of endurance events. Where they are permitted, five minutes of rest time are earned *after every completed hour* (full 60 minutes) of activity. These breaks can be accumulated so that, for example, after 3 hours of activity, 15 minutes of rest time would be earned. It is a good idea to keep some rest time in reserve so that you do not have to abandon your record attempt if something arises to delay your activity.

■

ABOUT VERIFICATION

Q. *I'm planning to try to break a world record. Will you send a Guinness representative to witness the attempt?*

A. No, Guinness does not send people to verify world records (the staff is just too busy), although we reserve the right to do so. You must assume the responsibility for proving that a world record has been set. The guidelines for submitting record claims to Guinness are described on page 9 of every recent edition of the Guinness book, U.S. edition. Basically, the requirements are: signed statements from independent, impartial, adult witnesses, as well as experts in the field of endeavor, log books for endurance events, and media coverage, (newspaper, radio, TV). Guinness cannot and will not accept a record that is insufficiently documented.

Q. *How do I arrange for media coverage?*

A. This is hardly ever a problem. Newspapers in particular, but also radio and TV stations, are usually happy to cover local record attempts and print successful results. You should be aware, however, that newspaper reporters are usually less demanding than Guinness when it comes to calling something a world record.

Q. *Who are acceptable as independent adult witnesses?*

A. These should be people of standing in your community and they may not be related to you or involved in your record attempt. Some examples might be the mayor of your town, a judge, a dean or professor at a nearby college, the president of the Lion's Club or Jaycees, or a minister from a local church or temple. If one or more of these witnesses has some expertise in the field of your endeavor so much the better. Be clever. The documentation for the world's largest pizza included a signed statement from the county's Commissioner of the Bureau of Weights and Measures, attesting to the accuracy of the measurements.

Q. *What should I include in the log book?*

A. The log book must show the times of activity and the times when breaks were taken (and the reasons), beginning at the start of the attempt and proceeding in order to the end. This way, the Guinness editors can see that you followed the rest-break rules. The log book must also contain signatures of witnesses to show that the event was witnessed by at least two people at every moment. Witnesses should sign their names and show the times entering and leaving, and their replacements should do the same. If your record involves playing a game, you should keep score sheets so Guinness can see that a satisfactory rate of play was maintained.

Q. *What else do I need to convince you?*

A. You should be very thorough and include as much specific information as possible. If weight or distance is a factor in your submission, tell how and who made your measurements. Remember that your task is to prove both the truth and accuracy of your claim. More "hard" information from you means fewer doubts in the minds of the Guinness investigators. Also, send action photographs in color or black-and-white to help illustrate your attempt. If the photos are interesting and reproducible, they will be included in the Guinness book if your record is accepted and space permits.

Q. *Where should I send everything?*

A. Send your record claim and documentation to: Guinness Book of World Records, Sterling Publishing Co., Two Park Avenue, New York, NY 10016. To help speed your claim, include copies of the main features of your documentation (but not copies of log books) so the New York office can keep information on file while your submission is forwarded to Guinness headquarters in England. Also, keep copies of everything for yourself in case of postal mishaps. Include a large enough self-addressed, stamped envelope to help the New York office reply to your claim, and send you special standards for some events.

Q. *How will I know whether or not my record has been accepted?*

A. Guinness will contact you, by mail, with the acceptance or rejection of your claim, or with a request for additional information. However, since the Guinness offices receive such a tremendous quantity of mail, it is impossible to investigate and respond to all claims immediately. If your claim is accepted you will receive a certificate. You must be patient—your submission will be answered. ■

GUINNESS WORLD RECORDS COME ALIVE IN CHAIN OF INTERNATIONAL MUSEUMS

Reading about Guinness World Records has been a fascinating experience for the more than 40 million people who have purchased the book, and untold millions more who have browsed over their shoulders or borrowed it from libraries all over the world. Quite an audience—one that represents all ages (from first graders to senior citizens), as well as all nationalities and socio-economic groups.

Would this vast audience be interested in visiting places where they could see actual record-breaking objects and films of records actually being set? David A. Boehm, the American publisher, and Norris McWhirter, the author of the Guinness Book, responsible for the worldwide Guinness popularity explosion, both thought so, and, in May 1976, the Guinness World Records Exhibit Hall was established in the Empire State Building.

Within four short years this simple concept—bringing the Guinness Book of World Records to life—proved to be so popular that six more Guinness Museums were established: from New York City across the United States to Fisherman's Wharf in San Francisco, California, up to Clifton Hill in Niagara Falls, Canada; south and west to Ocean Boulevard, Myrtle Beach, South Carolina; Lake of the Ozarks,

Missouri and Gatlinburg, Tennessee. Then across the ocean to Tivoli, Stockholm, Sweden.

And this is just the beginning. A new museum was opened near Mt. Fuji, Japan, in 1981. Within the next few years American Guinness Museums are planned for Baltimore, Chicago, Boston, Orlando, Dallas-Ft. Worth and Washington, D.C. In Scandinavia where the book is phenomonally popular a museum was opened in Helsinki. Paris, Oslo and Cologne are on the schedule for 1982 and London and Sydney for 1983.

It's a success story: one based on the blending of exciting exhibitry and prudent management, always striving to maintain the integrity of the Guinness name—being absolutely certain that everything on display has been fully researched and documented before it is accepted as an official record.

During your visit to a Guinness Museum, you will enjoy a unique multi-media show dramatizing the world's largest and smallest, zaniest and cleverest, most valuable, greatest, most unusual and fascinating records and record holders. The "Guinness Book of World Records" really does come to life with actual record-breaking objects, exciting audience participation devices, 3-dimensional presentations, sequential light displays, realistic replicas, and videotapes and films of amazing records actually being set.

You can see on tape the tallest man and tallest woman, the fattest twins, a man pulling a train with his teeth, great moments in sports, the famous domino tumbles, exciting highlights of Guinness TV shows and many, many more.

The Guinness museums fill a need that, for the most part, has been sorely neglected—providing exciting family and educational entertainment.

Thousands of school children have visited the museums on class trips and countless families have made a visit to Guinness a fun part of their leisure activity, many making repeat visits to see the new records that are constantly added to our exhibits.

So, if you haven't as yet visited one of the museums and plan to be near one of the locations, drop in. In fact, if you bring any issue of the Guinness Magazine, you will be given a special discount. ■

(Above, right) On Fisherman's Wharf, San Francisco, the Guinness Museum is just below DiMaggio's restaurant. In New York's Empire State Building, the Guinness Exhibit Hall, which has a twin-ticket plan with the Observatory, features video views of records being set, as do all the museums. (Below) Animal records are shown by slides in the museums in the south.

Scenes from the Gatlinburg Guinness Museum.

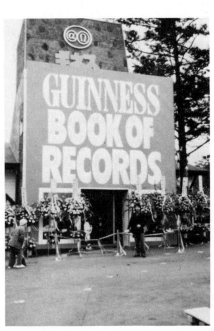

Tallest man and eating records and longest wig are featured in almost all Guinness Museums.
In Japan, the museum opening featured record balloon release. You enter through a door in a
giant book.